lo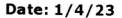

VIETNAM

Nguyen Le Diem, James Pham,

Scale, scamper and climb in the world's largest cave. Learn how coffee is made from seed to cup. Send paper models of luxury items as gifts to the dead. See how contemporary artists document Vietnam's past and present. Explore the country's largest Chinatown on a heritage walking tour. Sample cocktails and craft beers inspired by Vietnamese flavours. Cruise between river islands for a taste of quaint, countryside living. Slurp down a bowl of horse stew, a Hmong speciality. Muster the courage to abseil down waterfalls and slide down cliff faces.

This is Vietnam.

TURN THE PAGE AND START PLANNING YOUR NEXT BEST TRIP →

Street vendors, Hoi An (p118)

Joshua Zukas

@ *@joshuazukas*

British by birth, Joshua has considered Hanoi home since 2013. His ideal day in the city is spent hunting out street food for lunch, coffee shop hopping in the afternoon and cocktail bar crawling in the evening.

Contents

HUY THOAI/SHUTTERSTOCK ©

Halong Bay (p80)

Vietnam was forecasted to export 31.3 million 60kg bags of coffee in 2021–22.

Arabica beans account for only 4% to 5% of Vietnam's total coffee production.

The Vietnamese add condensed milk because under French rule fresh milk was hard to obtain.

COFFEE
CULTURE

▬▬ Introduced by the French in the late 1800s, coffee as a crop never really took off until nearly a century later when Vietnam became the world's number-two coffee-exporting country.

The Vietnamese also know how to enjoy their coffee: rich and dark, most often made in a metal drip filter with a healthy dose of condensed milk for a velvety smooth brew, hot or with ice.

→ COFFEE VARIATIONS

Be open to a range of speciality coffees, including coconut coffee (with coconut cream), egg coffee (with frothed egg yolk) and yogurt coffee (with plain yogurt).

Left Coffee plantation **Right** Egg coffee **Below** Vietnamese coffee brewed with metal filter

ORIGIN STORY

French missionaries originally brought the coffee plant to Vietnam in the mid-1800s. Vietnam is now a top-five coffee-exporting country, most of its output robusta beans.

↑ SLOW BREW

Vietnamese coffee is most commonly made in a metal filter and allowed to slowly drip into the cup with the addition of condensed milk.

Best Coffee Experiences

▶ Try an egg coffee (in which egg yolks replace milk) at Loading T in Hanoi. (p45)

▶ Cool off with a shaved-ice coconut-milk coffee at Hanoi's Cong Ca Phe. (p45)

▶ Visit the World of Coffee Museum in Dak Lak, Vietnam's biggest coffee-growing province. (p171)

▶ Learn about the entire coffee production process, from seed to cup, at the K'Ho Coffee Farm. (p168)

UNESCO BUCKET LIST

Part of Unesco's mission includes bringing attention to World Heritage Sites, intangible cultural heritage, geoparks and biosphere reserves of outstanding universal value. Vietnam is blessed with all of the above, from the enchanting islands of Halong Bay to the gongs of the central highlands that unite the physical and spiritual worlds, making these places a worthy addition to your itinerary.

Ha Giang
Cao Bang
Tuyen Quang
Yen Bai
Thai Nguyen
Viet Tri
✪ HANOI
Hoa Binh
Mai Chau
Thai Binh
Cuc Phuong National Park
Nam Soi
Ninh Binh
Thanh Hoa

LAOS

Nam Can

● **Vinh**

Cau Treo
Ha Tinh

Phong Nha-Ke Bang National Park

Son Doong Cave
World's largest cave
For experienced trekkers, exploring the world's largest cave is the ultimate bucket-list experience, requiring a 25km trek in the jungle and mountains, rope climbs, and scaling the 90m-high 'Great Wall of Vietnam'. For the less agile, smaller caves await.
🚗 *1hr from Dong Hoi Airport*
▶ p111

My Son
Ancient Cham temple towers
The Cham people ruled over parts of coastal Vietnam between the 4th and 13th centuries, with My Son as their religious and political capital. Step back in time strolling through this impressive collection of temple towers.
🚗 *1½hr from Hoi An*
▶ p118

THAILAND

0 ——— 200 km
0 ——— 100 miles

CHINA

Lang Son

Dong Van Karst Plateau
Gorgeous mountains and canyons
The spectacular landscape of high mountains and deep canyons of the Dong Van Karst Plateau is home to 17 ethnic minority groups. Trek through this ancient site dating back some 550 million years, visiting local villages and markets.

🚌 *10hr from Hanoi*

▶ p86

Halong City

Haiphong

Halong Bay
Cruise around ancient islets
Cruising around more than 1600 limestone islets (most uninhabited) that make up Halong Bay's spectacular seascape is truly unforgettable. Bonus activities include stops to explore caves, kayaking the emerald waters and lazing on picture-perfect beaches.

🚙 *3hr from Hanoi*

▶ p80

Gulf of Tonkin

Dong Hoi

East Sea (South China Sea)

Dong Ha

Lao Bao

Bach Ma National Park • **Danang**

Hoi An

Tam Ky

Hoi An
Medieval port town
Arguably Vietnam's most photogenic town, Hoi An's exceptionally well-preserved old town, lined by clay-tile-roofed shophouses, is a wonderful mix of cultural influences from when it was a busy trading port between the 15th and 19th centuries.

🚙 *1hr from Danang*

▶ p118

Street art is relatively new to Vietnam, although it's becoming increasingly mainstream. Much of it revolves around environmental themes and tourism rather than political ideology.

GEKKO GALLERY/SHUTTERSTOCK ©

Best Art Experiences

▶ Check out wartime propaganda art at HCMC's Museum of Fine Arts. (p189)

▶ Take in the nearly 4km-long Hanoi Ceramic Mosaic Mural depicting Vietnam's history. (p65)

▶ Learn how Vietnamese contemporary artists document social issues at HCMC's Craig Thomas Gallery. (p191)

▶ See Hanoi's extraordinary outdoor art project using recycled trash behind the Long Bien Market. (p65)

ART
APPRECIATION

■■■■ Vietnam has a rich history of traditional art, from the famous Dong Son drums of the Bronze Age to calligraphy and lacquer art influenced by Chinese rule to works of art using traditional mediums like silk, lacquer and oil but with European techniques, thanks to the French. In recent years, street and contemporary art are giving a new means of expression to Vietnamese artists.

HISTORY
HOUNDS

Vietnam has a long history marked by conflict and colonisation. For more than a millennium, China ruled parts of northern Vietnam while the French made the country part of their Indochina colony. Get a better sense of Vietnam's past by visiting notable museums and going on historic walks to witness the legacy of these outside influences.

Best Historical Experiences

▶ **Roam downtown Ho Chi Minh City** for a superb collection of heritage buildings. (p183)

▶ **Meet the leader most Vietnamese simply call 'Uncle'** at the Ho Chi Minh Museum. (p59)

▶ **Appreciate the female perspective** at the Vietnamese Women's Museum. (p59)

▶ **Explore the country's largest Chinatown**, with temple visits and dim sum eats. (p200)

← HUE & HANOI

Hue was Vietnam's capital under the Nguyen dynasty from 1802 to 1945.

2010 was the millennial anniversary of the founding of Hanoi (then called Thang Long).

Far left Hanoi Ceramic Mosaic Mural **Top left** Ho Chi Minh Museum, Hanoi **Bottom left** Central Post Office, HCMC

→ HERITAGE BUILDINGS

Almost every town in Vietnam has at least a few heritage buildings. Look for yellow walls, once favoured as a symbol of royalty and supremacy.

▶ Read about the fight to save Ho Chi Minh City's heritage buildings on p202

TOP VIETNAM STOCK IMAGES/SHUTTERSTOCK © BOTTOM WALTER BIBIKOW/GETTY IMAGES ©

Fansipan
Climb for amazing views

At 3143m high, Fansipan is Indochina's tallest peak. Test yourself with a challenging six- to eight-hour climb on steep, misty trails with views of forested valleys and mountains along the way. At the top, gaze out over the impressive Hoang Lien Son mountain range. The less adventurous can skip the two-day round-trip hike and take the 6km-long cable car instead.

🚌 *20min from Sapa*

▶ p82

OUTDOOR
ADVENTURES

▬▬ Vietnam's geography is incredibly diverse, from mountains in the north and the cool central highlands to the flat coastal lowlands of the delta regions. Vietnam also has over 3200km of coastline and at least 40 islands to explore. This all adds up to an amazing outdoor playground where trekking, camping, canyoning, hiking and more await.

Dalat Region
Canyoning down waterfalls

Dalat's natural beauty lies in its mountains, forests and waterfalls. Experience all three environments with an exhilarating day of canyoning, the ultimate adventure sport combining free jumping into pools, abseiling down waterfalls, sliding down cliff faces and more.

🚌 *15min from Dalat*

▶ p168

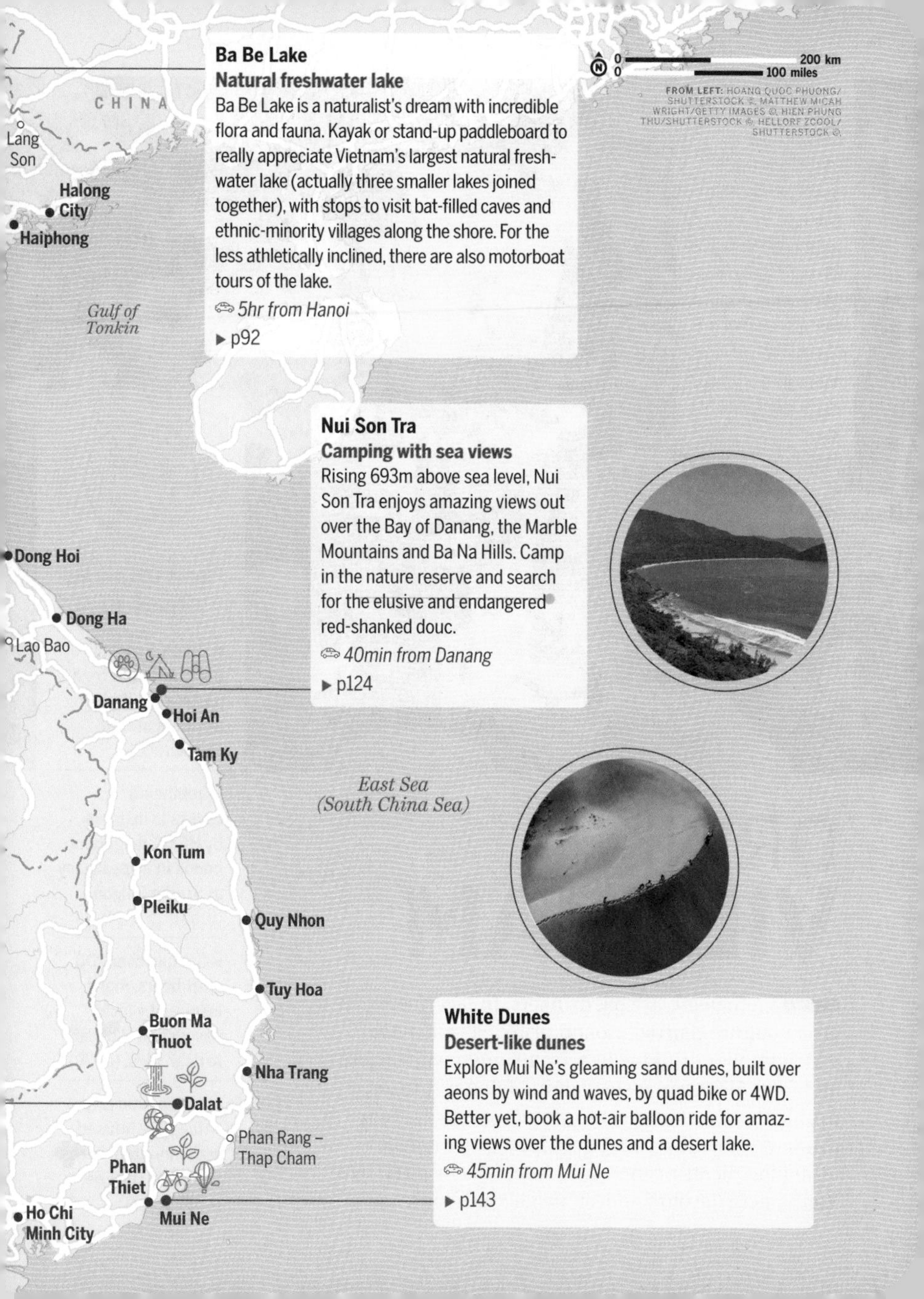

CHINA
Lang Son
Halong City
Haiphong
Gulf of Tonkin
Dong Hoi
Dong Ha
Lao Bao
Danang
Hoi An
Tam Ky
East Sea (South China Sea)
Kon Tum
Pleiku
Quy Nhon
Tuy Hoa
Buon Ma Thuot
Nha Trang
Dalat
Phan Rang – Thap Cham
Phan Thiet
Mui Ne
Ho Chi Minh City
0 200 km
0 100 miles

FROM LEFT: HOANG QUOC PHUONG/SHUTTERSTOCK ©, MATTHEW MICAH WRIGHT/GETTY IMAGES ©, HIEN PHUNG THU/SHUTTERSTOCK ©, HELLORF ZCOOL/SHUTTERSTOCK ©

Ba Be Lake

Natural freshwater lake

Ba Be Lake is a naturalist's dream with incredible flora and fauna. Kayak or stand-up paddleboard to really appreciate Vietnam's largest natural freshwater lake (actually three smaller lakes joined together), with stops to visit bat-filled caves and ethnic-minority villages along the shore. For the less athletically inclined, there are also motorboat tours of the lake.

5hr from Hanoi

▶ p92

Nui Son Tra

Camping with sea views

Rising 693m above sea level, Nui Son Tra enjoys amazing views out over the Bay of Danang, the Marble Mountains and Ba Na Hills. Camp in the nature reserve and search for the elusive and endangered red-shanked douc.

40min from Danang

▶ p124

White Dunes

Desert-like dunes

Explore Mui Ne's gleaming sand dunes, built over aeons by wind and waves, by quad bike or 4WD. Better yet, book a hot-air balloon ride for amazing views over the dunes and a desert lake.

45min from Mui Ne

▶ p143

In 2020, the annual average beer consumption in Vietnam was 40.5L per person.

Bia hoi, a very light draught beer brewed daily, is especially popular in northern Vietnam.

Vietnamese often drink beer with ice.

Best Drinking Experiences

▶ Go on a cocktail-bar crawl (and try a *pho* cocktail) hitting up spots around Hanoi. (p60)

▶ Imbibe on cocktails inspired by HCMC neighbourhoods in a speakeasy at Studio Saigon. (p195)

▶ Sample over 200 craft beers, many inspired by local flavours, at BiaCraft Artisan Ales. (p209)

▶ Sip on *ruou can*, a rice wine infused with mountain herbs picked by the Ede people. (p171)

DRINK
VIETNAM

━━ Vietnamese are big drinkers. In fact, there's an entire culture centred around drinking called *nhau*, which implies drinking in a group, often with snacks and food. However, instead of imbibing just to get drunk, there's a movement towards savouring your drink, whether it's a craft beer infused with hyper-local ingredients or innovative cocktails inspired by Vietnamese flavours or even neighbourhoods.

URBAN
NATURE

It's estimated that more than 80% of Vietnam's total land area is agricultural, meaning you don't need to go very far out of the city to find forests, farms, rivers and lakes. However, even in dense urban areas, you'll often find peaceful pockets of greenery to at least temporarily escape city life.

TOP: DUC HUY NGUYEN/SHUTTERSTOCK ©. BOTTOM: EVGENII MITROSHIN/SHUTTERSTOCK ©

→ PARK EXERCISE

Because homes are typically small, the Vietnamese love exercising in local parks, either walking, dancing, kicking around shuttlecocks or using the public gym equipment.

▶ Learn more about wellness in Vietnam on p172

Best Nature Experiences

▶ **Hop aboard Saigon's waterbus** for river views. (p196)

▶ **Wander the plantations of Banana Island** and perhaps stumble upon Hanoi's only nudist colony. (p52)

▶ **Walk around Dalat's Xuan Huong Lake** with stops for a swan-boat ride or coffee with lake views. (p162)

▶ **Explore river islands between My Tho and Ben Tre** for a taste of country living. (p221)

← CITIES ON WATER

Known as 'the city of lakes', Hanoi has at least 10 lakes within its city limits.

Meant for commuters, HCMC's waterbus is now more popular with tourists.

Far left *Nhau*, An Giang **Top left** Saigon Waterbus **Bottom left** Park exercises, HCMC

Pho was likely invented in the late 19th century in northern Vietnam.

Cao lau noodles are almost impossible to find outside Hoi An due to a unique combination of lye water and wood used to make them.

REGIONAL
EATS

Vietnamese food is so much more than *pho* and *banh mi* sandwiches. Each region has its own specialities based on different local products, thanks to its various climates and foreign influences, especially from China in the north as well as French ingredients and cooking techniques. Wherever you find yourself in Vietnam, eat hyper-local and enjoy the incredible culinary diversity Vietnam has to offer.

→ LOCAL TASTES

Vietnamese food in the north is more subtle and less meat-forward, dishes in the south are slightly sweeter, and central Vietnamese cuisine is the spiciest.

Left *Cao lau* **Right** *Pho cuon* **Below** Fried egg & baguette breakfast

KNOW BEFORE YOU GO

Vietnam's most popular online directory for restaurants is foody.vn. While only in Vietnamese, it's good for photos, menus and user-generated star ratings.

▶ Discover the restaurants at the forefront of innovative Vietnamese cuisine on p192

↑ ONE MORE MEAL

If your hotel breakfast spread isn't amazing, skip it and go for something tastier outside like a noodle soup or baguette with fried egg.

▶ Feast your eyes on an array of Vietnamese street food on p206

Best Food Experiences

▶ Sample Hanoi's *pho cuon*, fresh spring rolls stuffed with stir-fried beef. (p55)

▶ Dig into *thang co*, a traditional sweet, sour and salty horse stew of the Hmong people. (p97)

▶ Sit down to a bowl of *cao lau*, a thick noodle soup found only in Hoi An. (p115)

▶ Have a bowl of *bun mam*, noodle soup made from pickled fish in Can Tho. (p223)

▶ Pick your own seafood and have it cooked your way at Ham Ninh fishing village. (p233)

The finest lacquerware requires as many as 200 thin coats of lacquer and can incorporate eggshells, mother-of-pearl and gold leaf.

Hue is famous for conical hats which reveal lines of poetry when held up to the sun.

ARTS &
CRAFTS

Vietnam has over 1500 craft villages, some of which sprung up to serve the emperors around Hanoi and Hue. Artisans of the same craft often established these close-knit communities, only sharing their skills with family members or fellow villagers. In other cases, villagers turned to handicrafts during downtime between harvests, making use of ingenuity and locally available materials as a way of earning extra income.

Left Glass noodle production, Cu Da
Right Ceramic souvenirs, Bat Trang
Below Hmong woman sewing
traditional clothes

→ AUTHENTIC CRAFTS

Much of the souvenirs sold in markets are actually made in China. Visiting craft villages isn't just fascinating but assures you're getting something authentic.

REPRODUCTION ART

Many Vietnamese art students are skilled in reproducing masterpieces. You can even commission them to custom-paint a family portrait based on a photo.

▶ Find out where to find reproduction art in Ho Chi Minh City on p189

↑ ETHNIC APPEAL

Many of Vietnam's dozens of ethnic minority groups are known for their fine weaving, embroidery, batik and appliqué work, especially in northern Vietnam around Sapa.

▶ Marvel at the handiwork of northern Vietnamese ethnic groups at Bac Ha market (p94)

Best Artisanal Experiences

▶ **See how glass noodles are made in the photogenic village of Cu Da.** (p68)

▶ **Send the dead into the afterlife loaded with paper money and bling at Dao Tu village.** (p69)

▶ **Observe the work that goes into making Vietnam's most famous pottery at Bat Trang.** (p68)

▶ **Learn how chocolate is made from bean to bar at the Muoi Cuong Cacao Farm.** (p225)

↘ Ooc Om Bok

Dragon-boat races powered by 50 to 60 rowers per boat are the highlight of this lively Khmer festival in the 10th lunar month.

📍 Soc Trang province

↓ Dalat Flower Festival

This biennial festival (every odd year, December or January) showcases thousands of flowers around the main thoroughfares.

📍 Dalat

Demand for accommodation peaks during the months before and after Christmas. Book tours and overnight adventures in advance.

▶ lonelyplanet.com/vietnam/activities

NOVEMBER

Average daytime max: 26°C /
Days of rainfall: 16 (Hue)

DECEMBER

Average daytime max: 23°C /
Days of rainfall: 17 (Hue)

Vietnam in
DRY SEASON

↘ Cruising the Delta

Consider taking a boat cruise as flowers are coaxed to bloom for Tet, making for extremely colourful floating markets.

📍Mekong Delta

▶ p228

↗ Lim Festival

Taking place in the first lunar month, this colourful festival features Unesco-inscribed Quan Ho folk singing.

📍Bac Ninh

JANUARY

Average daytime max: 23°C /
Days of rainfall: 14 (Hue)

FEBRUARY

Average daytime max: 24°C /
Days of rainfall: 10 (Hue)

← Tet Nguyen Dan

Expect week-long business closures and inflated prices during Vietnamese Lunar New Year in late January or early February,

Packing Notes

If travelling to northern Vietnam or the central highlands, pack a jacket as places like Sapa can see snow and frost.

↓ Buon Ma Thuot Coffee Festival

Visit Vietnam's coffee-growing capital in March as the coffee bushes come into bloom and everything coffee-related is celebrated.

📍 Buon Ma Thuot

▶ p170

↗ Phu Day Festival

Colourful processions, singing, dancing and religious rites mark this festival worshipping Mother Goddess in the third lunar month.

📍 Nam Dinh province

↓ Hue Festival

Taking place in April every two (even) years, this week-long festival features cultural events, traditional games and performances.

📍 Hue

▶ huefestival.com

MARCH

Average daytime max: 27°C / Days of rainfall: 9 (Hue)

APRIL

Vietnam in
SHOULDER
SEASON

↘ Khau Vai Love Market

This century-old ethnic market features cultural activities, folk games, and a food fest in the third lunar month.

📍 Ha Giang province

▶ p100

↗ Hot, dry days are perfect for beach destinations like Danang, Nha Trang, Mui Ne and Phu Quoc.

MAY

Average daytime max: 29°C / Days of rainfall: 9 (Hue)

Average daytime max: 31°C / Days of rainfall: 16 (Hue)

Demand for accommodation peaks around 30 April (Reunification Day) and 1 May (Labour Day). Book tours and overnight adventures in advance.

▸ lonelyplanet.com/vietnam/activities

🧳 Packing Notes

Pack for warm weather and bring sunscreen. If you're prone to excessive sweating, prickly-heat powder is your friend.

Demand for accommodation peaks during June through August. Book tours and overnight adventures in advance.

▶ lonelyplanet.com/vietnam/activities

↓ Kate Festival

The highlight of the year for the Cham people, in the seventh lunar month, with the largest celebration at the ancient temple towers.

📍 Phan Rang

▶ p138

↗ Fruit Season

June to August is a great time to visit the delta during the height of the fruit-harvesting season, especially in Vinh Long, Cai Be and Ben Tre.

📍 Mekong Delta

JUNE	JULY	AUGUST
Average daytime max: 32°C / Days of rainfall: 14 (Hue)	Average daytime max: 32°C / Days of rainfall: 14 (Hue)	

Vietnam in
RAINY
SEASON

↓ Mid-Autumn Festival

A post-harvest festival in September or October, popular with children – expect lots of colourful lanterns, especially in Hoi An.

● Hoi An

↗ Turtle-Nesting Season

From June to September, visit Bay Canh Island in Con Dao to see turtles laying their eggs in the sand.

● Con Dao archipelago

▶ p148

SEPTEMBER

Average daytime max: 31°C /
Days of rainfall: 14 (Hue)

Average daytime max: 30°C /
Days of rainfall: 17 (Hue)

OCTOBER

Average daytime max: 27°C /
Days of rainfall: 18 (Hue)

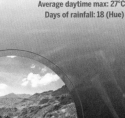

↘ Excellent time to visit Sapa, when the rice terraces turn a beautiful golden colour ready for harvesting.

● Sapa

▶ p86

 Packing Notes

Bring plastic shoes or sandals and insect repellent. Single-use plastic ponchos are sold everywhere.

NORTHERN VIETNAM
Trip Builder

TAKE YOUR PICK OF MUST-SEES AND HIDDEN GEMS

Hanoi is a delightful capital with colonial French-era buildings, ancient pagodas and world-class museums within the Old Quarter's craft streets. From Hanoi, explore the north's other-worldly islands and stunning mountains, and meet fascinating ethnic minority groups.

🗺 Trip Notes

Hub town Hanoi

How long Allow 10 days

Getting around From Hanoi, buses and minivans are the best options to get to the northern destinations. Halong Bay cruises have the option to include shuttle transfer directly to your boat and back.

Tips Save a hotel night each way by travelling to Sapa via night train. To avoid the crowds in Halong Bay, consider a longer two- or three-night cruise.

Bac Ha
See a colourful cross-section of various minority groups decked out in their finest garb at Vietnam's largest ethnic market trading in brocade, farming tools, horses and buffalo.
🚌 4hr from Sapa

Bac Ha

Mt Fansipan

Lao Cai

Sapa

Bac Ngam

Hoang Lien National Park

Trai Hut

Sapa
Conquer Fansipan, Indochina's highest peak, and trek the centuries-old terraced rice fields built by the hill-tribes people in this former colonial-era hill station.
🚆 7hr from Hanoi

Van An

Ba Khe

Ban Pho

Chieng Pan

Moc Chau

LAOS

0   50 km
0   25 miles

Ha Giang
Drive along incredibly scenic passes laboriously carved into the mountains overlooking plunging valleys, impossibly steep farm fields and rustic minority villages.
🚆 7hr from Hanoi

Ba Be Lake
Experience the beauty of Vietnam's largest natural lake by kayaking, stand-up paddleboarding and camping, with time to explore caves, waterfalls, island temples and local villages.
🚆 7hr from Hanoi

Hanoi
Discover secret cocktail bars and thought-provoking street art in Vietnam's 1000-year-old capital, home to an amazing art and music scene and where coffee drinking is an obsession.
🚆 7hr from Sapa

Halong Bay
Cruise, kayak and swim the gorgeous seascapes of this Unesco-listed World Heritage Site where over 1600 mostly uninhabited, jungle-clad islands rise from emerald waters.
🚢 3hr from Hanoi

Tam Son

CHINA

Ha Giang

Cao Bang

Tan Quang

Ba Be National Park

Na Phac

Bac Kan

Thac Lake

Tuyen Quang

Yen Bai

Lang Son

Bien Dong

Tien Yen

Viet Tri

Vinh Yen

Bac Giang

Halong City

Cam Pha

HANOI

Song Da Reservoir

Hoa Binh

Haiphong

Cat Ba Island

Mai Chau

Phu Nho Quan

Cam Thuy

CENTRAL VIETNAM
Trip Builder

TAKE YOUR PICK OF MUST-SEES AND HIDDEN GEMS

▬▬▬ Central Vietnam is full of history, culture and opportunities to relax on a pretty beach with a fresh coconut in hand. From historic Hoi An to the long stretches of beach in Danang to the majestic caves of Phong Nha, there's something for everyone.

🗺 Trip Notes

Hub towns Danang, Hue

How long Allow two weeks

Getting around Danang makes for a great base with air, train and bus connections and easy access to Hoi An, My Son and Hue.

Tips If Son Doong's price tag seems a bit hefty, Phong Nha has lots of other caves to explore on a budget. Time your trip to Hoi An for the monthly Lantern Festival.

Son Doong
Trek through the planet's largest cave, scaling a 90m-high calcite barrier, walking through subterranean rainforests and swimming in underground rivers.
🚆 *4hr from Hue*

Vinh

Ha Tinh

Ky Anh

Cha Lo

Quang Trach

Phong Nha-Ke Bang National Park

Dong Hoi

Demilitarised Zone (DMZ)

Lao Bao

Danang
Enjoy a winning combination of city comforts and beautiful beaches, and go camping in a nature reserve, hunting for secret waterfalls and spotting the endangered red-shanked douc.
🚆 *2½hr from Hue*

LAOS

CHINA

East Sea
(South China Sea)

Hue
Explore a curated selection of royal tombs on a cycling or motorbike adventure around this former imperial capital of Vietnam.
🚆 2½hr from Danang

Hoi An
Walk back in time through Hoi An's beautifully preserved old town filled with atmospheric temples, colourful lanterns and artfully aged shophouses.
🚌 1hr from Danang

My Son
Wander around dozens of ancient temple towers featuring stone pillars and sandstone reliefs built over 10 centuries.
🚐 1½hr from Hoi An

○ Ben Hai

● Dong Ha

Hue

Bach Ma National Park

Danang

Cham Islands

● Hoi An

Ben Giang ○

Phuoc Son ○

Tam Ky

THE HIGHLANDS & THE SOUTHEAST COAST
Trip Builder

TAKE YOUR PICK OF MUST-SEES AND HIDDEN GEMS

▬▬▬ This region beautifully showcases Vietnam's incredible diversity, from the mountains and lakes of the central highlands, where coffee and flowers are grown, to the lovely beaches of the southeast coast – all within a few hours of each other.

🗺 Trip Notes

Hub towns Dalat, Nha Trang

How long Allow 10 days

Getting around Most of these destinations have their own airport, but buses and minivans are good options to get between the cities.

Tips With little traffic, Phan Thiet and Buon Ma Thuot are great for renting a motorbike. Book your bus ticket to Mui Ne (instead of Phan Thiet) to be dropped off at your hotel along the way.

CAMBODIA

Buon Ma Thuot
Learn all about coffee production from berry to brew in Vietnam's coffee-growing capital, where museums and farm workshops celebrate everyone's favourite bean.
🚌 *6hr from Dalat*

Dak Mil

Gia Nghia

Cat Tien National Park

Phan Thiet & Mui Ne
Go on a driving itinerary along the coast taking in ancient ruins, colourful canyons and towering sand dunes, with a stop along the way for fresh seafood.
🚌 *4hr from Ho Chi Minh City*

Pleiku

Binh
Dinh

N 0 ━━━━━━━━━━ 50 km
   0 ━━━━━━━━━━ 25 miles

Quy Nhon
Laze on some of Vietnam's best
stretches of sand in this off-the-
radar seaside city famous for its
fresh seafood, dramatic beaches
and ancient ruins.
🚆 *6hr from Danang*

Quy Nhon

A Yun Pa

Song Cau

Ea H'Leo

Tuy Hoa

Krong
Buk

Ban Don

Yok Don
National
Park
Buon Ma Thuot

M' Drak

Van Ninh

Ea T'Ling

Lien Son

*Chu Yang Sin
National Park*

Ninh Hoa

Nha Trang

Nha Trang
Slip and slide in a mineral
mud bath at Vietnam's
leading beach destina-
tion, known for cheap
island-hopping trips and a
family-friendly vibe.
🚆 *4hr from Dalat*

Dalat

Cam Ranh

*East Sea
(South China Sea)*

Dalat
Hike through the fragrant pine
forests of this French-era hillside
retreat that abounds in outdoor
activities like trekking, mountain
biking and canyoning down
waterfalls.
🚆 *4hr from Nha Trang*

Bao Loc

Phan Rang–
Thap Cham

Ca Na

Phan Rang
Join the Kate Festival,
the largest celebration of
Vietnam's Cham people, with
music, dancing and offerings
centred around the ancient
temple towers.
🚆 *2hr from Nha Trang*

Mui Ne

**Phan
Thiet**

SOUTHERN VIETNAM & THE MEKONG DELTA
Trip Builder

TAKE YOUR PICK OF MUST-SEES AND HIDDEN GEMS

▬▬▬ Vibrant and wonderfully chaotic, Ho Chi Minh City is a great place to start or end your trip, while overnight forays through the lush Mekong Delta showcase what life is like for most Vietnamese. Busy Phu Quoc and sedate Con Dao offer gorgeous beach getaways.

🗺 Trip Notes

Hub town Ho Chi Minh City

How long Allow 10 days

Getting around All buses and planes leave from Ho Chi Minh City. Motorbike taxis are quick and cheap in the cities, but opt for taxis on the islands.

Tips Pack light as the budget-airline tickets only allow carry-on. After travelling through the Mekong Delta, consider heading on to Cambodia by boat or bus or Phu Quoc by ferry.

0 — 50 km
0 — 25 miles

Chau Doc
Get a peek into life lived on and by the river with a boat trip to floating fish farms and a floating market, all surrounded by Khmer, Cham and Chinese communities.
🚌 *5hr from Ho Chi Minh City*

Xa Xia

Ha Tien

Phu Quoc Island

Duong Dong

Can Tho
Jostle among boats laden with fruit and vegetables at the largest floating market in the Mekong Delta, and eat your way through the region's array of specialities.
🚌 *4hr from Ho Chi Minh City*

Gulf of Thailand

Phu Quoc
Laze around on powdery beaches bordering turquoise waters. See the sunset from 19 storeys up, or take a scenic cable-car ride to an island paradise.
✈ *75min from Ho Chi Minh City*

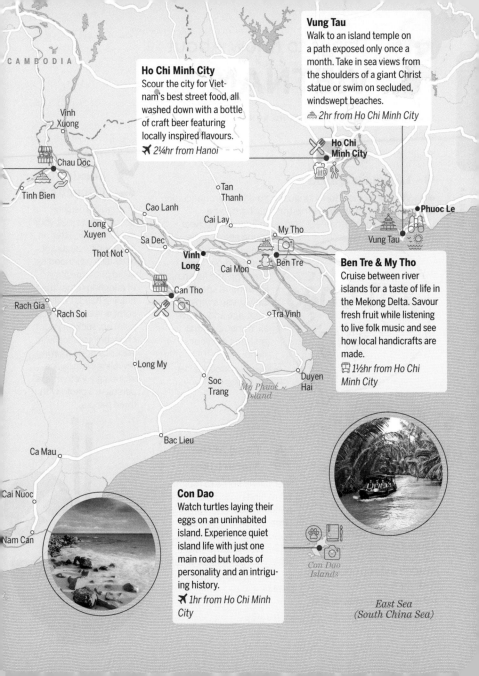

CAMBODIA

Ho Chi Minh City
Scour the city for Vietnam's best street food, all washed down with a bottle of craft beer featuring locally inspired flavours.
✈ 2¼hr from Hanoi

Vung Tau
Walk to an island temple on a path exposed only once a month. Take in sea views from the shoulders of a giant Christ statue or swim on secluded, windswept beaches.
⛴ 2hr from Ho Chi Minh City

Vinh Xuong

Chau Doc

Tinh Bien

Tan Thanh

Cao Lanh

Cai Lay

My Tho

Ho Chi Minh City

Phuoc Le

Long Xuyen

Sa Dec

Vinh Long

Cai Mon

Ben Tre

Vung Tau

Thot Not

Rach Gia

Can Tho

Rach Soi

Tra Vinh

Ben Tre & My Tho
Cruise between river islands for a taste of life in the Mekong Delta. Savour fresh fruit while listening to live folk music and see how local handicrafts are made.
🚐 1½hr from Ho Chi Minh City

Long My

Soc Trang

Duyen Hai

Mỹ Phước Island

Ca Mau

Bac Lieu

Cai Nuoc

Con Dao
Watch turtles laying their eggs on an uninhabited island. Experience quiet island life with just one main road but loads of personality and an intriguing history.
✈ 1hr from Ho Chi Minh City

Nam Can

Con Dao Islands

East Sea
(South China Sea)

7 Things to Know About
VIETNAM

INSIDE TIPS TO HIT THE GROUND RUNNING

1 Language Quirks

Vietnamese is a tonal language, so if your pronunciation is even slightly off, it can be frustratingly hard to be understood. The Vietnamese also learn English in school from a young age, but the focus leans towards grammar more than speaking and listening. Be patient, speak slowly, use simple language and, above all, remember that gestures are your friend.

▶ Read more about the Vietnamese language on p252

2 Local Etiquette

Though it's usually acceptable to pick your nose in public, litter on the floor in restaurants and slurp your noodles, avoid public displays of affection (other than holding hands), calling someone over with your palm up, sticking your chopsticks vertically in your rice bowl, wearing revealing clothing, or including a Vietnamese person in a photo with three people.

3 Plastic Money

Vietnam uses colourful banknotes. Double-check when using the 20,000d and 500,000d notes (similar shades of blue), and the 10,000d and 200,000d notes (both tan).

▶ See more about money on p245

4 Land of the Motorbikes

Vietnam is home to roughly 50 million motorbikes – the handiest way to get around. Grab, Gojek and Bee are popular ride-sharing apps. When crossing the street, raise your hand to be visible.

▶ See our motorbiking checklist on p123

5 Shopping Tips

Many Vietnamese sellers believe the first customer of the day portends how sales will go, so it's bad luck if the first customer doesn't make a purchase. Save your browsing for later in the day and, if bargaining, do it in a friendly spirit with a smile. Losing your temper or getting aggressive are signs of weakness.

6 Getting Around 101

While it's tempting to try and create an itinerary that encompasses the length of Vietnam in one to two weeks, factors such as distance, heat and the language barrier make getting from place to place a potentially exhausting task. Budget airlines can make travelling by air a cheap time saver, especially via regional airports with minimal procedures. Open bus tickets are economical, but you might be sacrificing sleep quality as the beds in sleeper buses are tight – those taller than 1.7m will likely feel cramped, with no way of stretching out. When travelling between cities on routes of five hours or less, check if there's a more comfortable minivan option.

Heat and humidity mean locals rarely walk any considerable distances. Save your walking for attractions grouped closely together and for cool mornings or late afternoons. Otherwise, do yourself a favour and catch a motorbike taxi instead.

▶ Learn more about getting around on p242

VIETNAM LOCAL TIPS

7 COVID-19

Vietnam has had a stellar record in dealing with the pandemic, with high vaccination rates and excellent communication with its citizens. You'll feel comfortable wearing masks here as locals have long done it, especially for pollution while driving. To date, the government has responded quickly to contain infection clusters, sometimes restricting travel to/from high-risk areas with little to no notice. For the latest info, check vietnam.travel.

▶ Read more about safe travel in Vietnam on p244

Read, Listen, Watch & Follow

 READ

Eat Vietnam
(Barbara Adam &
James Pham; 2021)
A compendium of
Vietnamese cuisine
and the stories
behind the food.

**The Quiet
American** (Graham
Greene; 1955) A love
triangle set in 1950s
Vietnam as the
French exit and the
Americans enter.

**Vietnam: Rising
Dragon** (Bill Hayton;
2010) An analysis
of international
relations and
economic
challenges.

**Exploring Saigon-
Cho Lon** (Tim
Doling; 2019) Part
of a series of guides
(including DIY
walking tours) by a
local historian.

 LISTEN

**The Voice of
Vietnam** (vovworld.
vn) State-run
English-language
broadcasts on
economics, culture,
society and more.

**What About
Vietnam** Podcast
host Kerry
Newsome covers
the whens and
hows of travelling to
Vietnam.

m-tp M-TP (Son
Tung; 2017) A
compilation
album from one
of Vietnam's most
successful artists,
dubbed the 'Prince
of V-pop'.

A Vietnam Podcast
Host Niall Mackay
talks to interesting
personalities about
their connection to
Vietnam.

Trinh Cong Son
Vietnam's beloved, prolific songwriter of
the 1960s and '70s with lyrics about love
and national reunification.

▷ WATCH

Rom (2019) Follow a 14-year-old bookie trying to make it on the streets of Ho Chi Minh City.

Cyclo (1995; pictured top right) A look into the hard life of a *cyclo* driver in 1990s Ho Chi Minh City.

Monsoon (2019; pictured bottom right) A British-Vietnamese man's personal journey to connect to the country of his birth.

Luke Nguyen's Vietnam (2010–11) Food documentary following Vietnamese-Australian celebrity chef's travels.

Full Metal Jacket (1987) War drama about the experiences of US Marines during the American War in Vietnam.

UNITED ARCHIVES GMBH /ALAMY STOCK PHOTO ©

LANDMARK MEDIA /ALAMY STOCK PHOTO ©

⊙ FOLLOW

Vietnam Coracle
(vietnamcoracle.com) Comprehensive, independent travel guide.

@Saigoneer
Food, travel, arts and culture.

Vietnam Tourism
(vietnam.travel) Well-written articles give a good overview of travel in Vietnam.

@HanoiGrapevine
Art and culture happenings in Hanoi.

Rusty Compass
(rustycompass.com) Well-researched travel guide to destinations across Vietnam.

⟋ Sate your Vietnam dreaming with a virtual vacation at lonelyplanet.com/vietnam# planning

HANOI

CULTURE | STREET-FOOD | URBAN DISCOVERY

Experience
Hanoi online

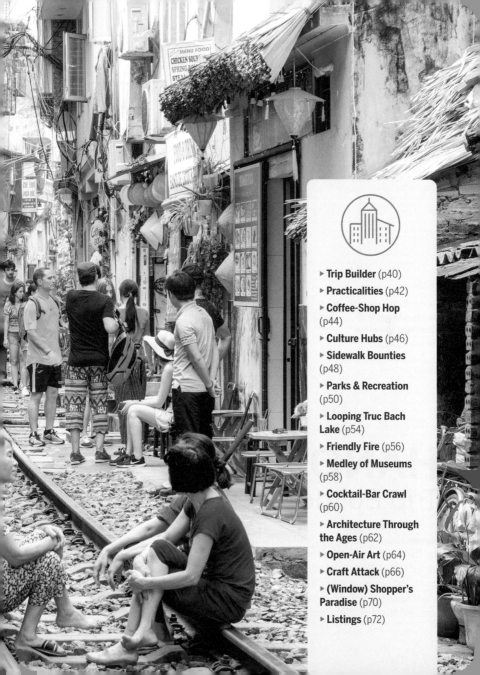

N
0 ─────────── 1 km
0 ─────────── 0.5 miles

*West Lake
(Ho Tay)*

Meander through leafy
streets and circle placid
ponds in **West Lake** (p53)
🚶 *15min from Hoan Kiem
Lake*

Get under the skin of
Hanoi's contempo-
rary art and music
scenes at **Manzi**
(p47)
🚶 *5min from Hoan
Kiem Lake*

To Lich River

Delve into the colourful
**Vietnam Museum of
Ethnology**, one of the
country's best (p59)
🚗 *20min from Temple of
Literature*

*Giang
Vo Lake*

*Dong Da
Lake*

HANOI
Trip Builder

▬▬▬ Hanoi is a city of wild extremes, evidenced
by the frenetic Old Quarter and laid-back lakes, the
ramshackle French Quarter and the modern business
districts. It's also a city of culture and creativity, with
craft villages, superb museums, artisanal hubs, street
art and thriving food, cafe and cocktail scenes.

**Explore bookable
experiences in
Hanoi**

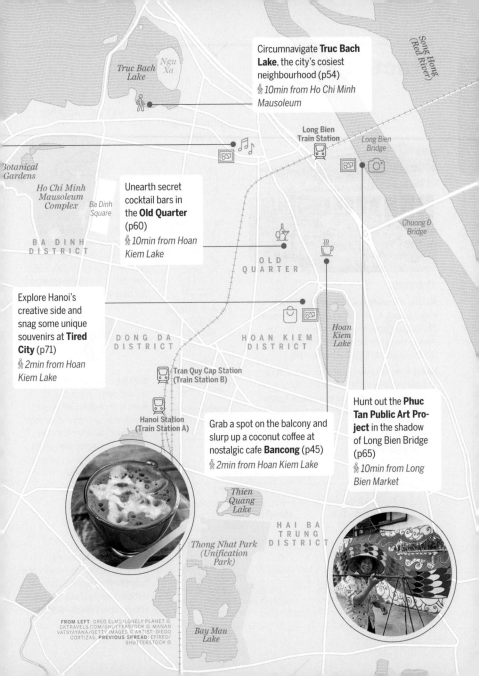

Circumnavigate **Truc Bach Lake**, the city's cosiest neighbourhood (p54)
🚶 10min from Ho Chi Minh Mausoleum

Unearth secret cocktail bars in the **Old Quarter** (p60)
🚶 10min from Hoan Kiem Lake

Explore Hanoi's creative side and snag some unique souvenirs at **Tired City** (p71)
🚶 2min from Hoan Kiem Lake

Grab a spot on the balcony and slurp up a coconut coffee at nostalgic cafe **Bancong** (p45)
🚶 2min from Hoan Kiem Lake

Hunt out the **Phuc Tan Public Art Project** in the shadow of Long Bien Bridge (p65)
🚶 10min from Long Bien Market

Truc Bach Lake

Ngu Xa

Song Hong (Red River)

Long Bien Train Station

Long Bien Bridge

Botanical Gardens

Ho Chi Minh Mausoleum Complex

Ba Dinh Square

BA DINH DISTRICT

Chuong Đ Bridge

OLD QUARTER

Hoan Kiem Lake

DONG DA DISTRICT

HOAN KIEM DISTRICT

Tran Quy Cap Station (Train Station B)

Hanoi Station (Train Station A)

Thien Quang Lake

HAI BA TRUNG DISTRICT

Thong Nhat Park (Unification Park)

Bay Mau Lake

Practicalities

ARRIVING

Noi Bai International Airport Hanoi's only major airport. A taxi to the centre costs around 350,000d; always request the meter. Bus 86 goes to the centre before the train station; buy tickets on board (30,000d per person).

Hanoi Train Station The central station. A taxi to a central hotel costs around 100,000d; a motorbike taxi is half that, but you have to bargain. Buses may drop you at one of the stations, most of which aren't central.

HOW MUCH FOR A

simple meal
50,000d

glass of draught beer (*bia hoi*)
10,000d

cyclo journey
200,000d

GETTING AROUND

Taxis and motorbike taxis Plentiful and cheap; journeys will rarely cost more than 100,000d. Consider downloading Grab (the Uber of Southeast Asia), which is clear and easy to use. You'll also spot *cyclos* (bicycle rickshaws) – but bargain hard.

Walking Hanoi's neighbourhoods are somewhat conducive to walking, though expect drivers to weave around you rather than stop to let you cross the road. Bicycles and motorbikes aren't recommended unless you're an expert on two wheels.

Public transport Hanoi's confusing public bus network and inconveniently located sky-train stations (from a visitor's point of view) aren't usually worth the hassle.

WHEN TO GO

FEB–APR
Cool but can be unpleasantly wet for days at a time.

MAY–AUG
Hot, sunny, with occasional downpours. Generally good air quality.

SEP–OCT
Lingering summer warmth, infrequent typhoons. High humidity.

NOV–JAN
Cold and dry. A good time to visit, though pollution can be a problem.

EATING & DRINKING

It's hard to exhaust the local delicacies in Hanoi. *Cha ca* (crispy fried fish with noodles; pictured top right) is a distinctly Hanoian dish found in speciality restaurants. Popular Hanoi-specific street food includes *bun cha*, *banh cuon* (pictured bottom right) and *pho cuon*. The *pho* here tastes totally different to the southern version. *Bia hoi* (draught beer) is a distinctly northern phenomenon, and Hanoi does it best. Expansive food menus are offered alongside the beer. Like the rest of Vietnam, Hanoi is obsessed with coffee, and you'll find a multitude of cafes on virtually every street.

Best coffee selection

Bancong (p45)

Must-try pho

Pho Gia Truyen Bat Dan

CONNECT & FIND YOUR WAY

Wi-fi and data Restaurants and cafes will have free and decent wi-fi. Pick up a SIM card with data at the airport or at phone stores; ask the sales assistant to register it for you.

Navigation Addresses can be confusing, but the pin on Google maps is usually correct.

WHERE TO STAY

Hanoi is something of a boutique-hotel mecca, with hundreds of well-located establishments offering friendly service at good prices.

Neighbourhood	Pro/Con
Hoan Kiem	The Old Quarter and surroundings. Widest range of options and competitive prices; variable quality.
Hai Ba Trung	The French Quarter. Plenty of restaurants and cafes; not many hotel options.
Tay Ho	Also known as West Lake. Expat enclave with a good international food scene. You need a taxi for most points of interest.
Ba Dinh	Including Truc Bach. Central and close to the major sites; not many hotel options.
My Dinh	Hanoi's CBD. Sleek hotels with easy access to the airport; expensive and a little soulless.

MONEY

Carry cash for cheap eats, coffee, markets and taxis. Cards are accepted in a growing number of places, but don't rely on it. ATMs are everywhere.

CROSSING THE ROAD

Much of your time will be spent walking, so it's imperative to learn early how to cross the road. If you're finding it daunting, ask a local to help.

01

Coffee-Shop
HOP

COFFEE | PEOPLE-WATCHING | WALKING

■■■ There's a new city competing to be the world's cafe capital – and it's not where you'd expect. Hanoi's historic cafe culture, blended with the global third-wave coffee movement, has brewed a diverse selection of cafes across the capital, from mom-and-pop street stalls to art-filled espresso bars. The Old Quarter is the best place to get stuck in.

🗺 How to

Getting around The Old Quarter is entirely walkable, so there's no need to brave a vehicle.

What to drink Along with Western favourites using quality local beans, there's a whole host of indigenous creations. Not into the black stuff? You'll also find tea, juices and smoothies.

When to drink Do as the Vietnamese do and drink coffee whenever you want. Most cafes are open from early morning until late in the evening.

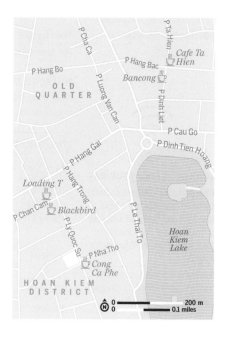

The local experience Taking time out to nurse a cup of local coffee surrounded by nattering locals is an essential Hanoi experience. The French introduced cafe culture to Vietnam, but the Vietnamese have since made it their own. It doesn't matter where you are in the country – a fresh cup of coffee is never more than a few steps away. Hanoi has one of the highest concentrations of cafes in Vietnam, but it also offers the most remarkable variety.

Summer refreshment Coconut coffee, which uses shaved-ice coconut milk, was

Top right Cafe Ta Hien **Bottom right** Traditional Vietnamese coffee

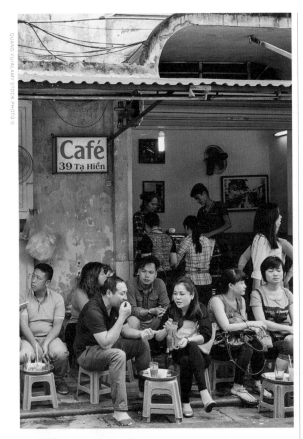

🔭 Bird's-Eye View

Serving all the coffees listed here and more, **Bancong** inhabits an unusually large art-deco building right in the centre of the Old Quarter. Grab a spot on one of the balconies and watch life unfold below.

probably invented at **Cong Ca Phe** (there are many branches around town but try 27 P Nha Tho), where gentle lighting and communist memorabilia hark back to Vietnam's pre-capitalist days. For traditional iced coffee served right on the street, squat knee to knee at **Cafe Ta Hien**.

Winter delights Egg coffee, which uses egg yolks instead of milk, is one of Hanoi's stranger coffees; it's also one of the most delicious. Scoop it up at **Loading T**, in a grandiose French-colonial mansion. For espresso-based coffees, try **Blackbird**, which balances hipster chic and Hanoi charm. You'll find standard hot Vietnamese coffee, sometimes served above a tea light to keep warm, in all the above establishments.

02 Culture **HUBS**

VISUAL ART | LIVE MUSIC | WORKSHOPS

▬▬▬ Hanoi is Vietnam's cultural capital, and that applies to contemporary culture as much as to past heritage. Despite government suspicion about free expression, an assortment of cultural hubs powered by creative youths thrives across the city, usually amalgamating temporary exhibition spaces, curated gift shops, venues for live music and trendy cafes or bars.

PAUL QUAYLE/ALAMY STOCK PHOTO ©

📷 How to

How to visit You can work some of these hubs into your sightseeing itineraries, as they sit near tourist hotspots. You'll need to make individual trips for the others.

Booking If you're dropping in for coffee, food or to shop, there's no need to tell them you're coming.

Events Check the venues' social media accounts for an events schedule and exhibition information. Book beforehand; messaging them on Facebook or Instagram will usually suffice.

REUTERS/ALAMY STOCK PHOTO ©

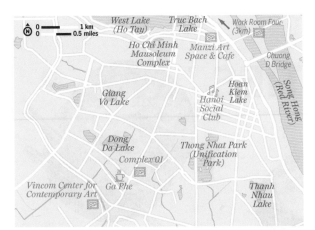

Top left Hanoi Social Club **Bottom left** Land Genie by Pham Thai Binh, Vincom Center for Contemporary Art

Many artsy cafes offer a range of decent adjunct cultural activities. For temporary exhibitions, film evenings and a superb contemporary art shop, head to **Manzi Art Space & Cafe**, north of the Old Quarter. For excellent coffee, drawing workshops and a window into Vietnamese comic-book culture, hunt out **Ga Phe** (20 Ngo 7 Thai Ha). For cosy, thoughtful evenings of live music mixed with a creative, global dinner menu, check out **Hanoi Social Club**, spread across three levels in a quiet laneway.

Other contemporary-art hubs include **Work Room Four** and **Manzi Exhibition Space** (just around the corner from its namesake cafe), which collaborate once or twice a year for ART For You, Hanoi's only affordable art fair. The **Vincom Center for Contemporary Art** is Hanoi's sleekest art gallery.

Buried down an alleyway, **Complex 01** (29 Ngach 31 Ngo 167 Tay Son) is a new collective of fashion ateliers, interior designers, creative agencies and juice bars. The hub still has room to grow so you'll find lots of empty space, but it should evolve quickly.

The **French Cultural Centre** (L'Espace) and the **Goethe Institute** from Germany are the city's most active international cultural associations, organising live music events, film festivals and art exhibitions.

ART For You

If you happen to be visiting towards the end of the year (check manziart. space for specific dates) and you want to explore the local art scene, you should definitely check out ART For You – the only affordable art fair in Vietnam. Manzi Art Space and Work Room Four launched the fair in 2014 with the goal of remunerating burgeoning artists and supporting independent art spaces in Hanoi. Each fair features more than 200 artists and showcases over 400 pieces priced from US$25 to US$900. This is a rare chance for buyers to scope out new talent or bring back work by an established contemporary artist.

■ **Recommended by Tram Vu,** co-founder of Manzi Art Space & Cafe @manzihn

Sidewalk
BOUNTIES

01 *Pho bo*

The classic Vietnamese noodle soup, beef *pho* is usually served with a range of cuts, from lean slivers to juicy chunks.

02 *Pho ga*

Pho is so iconic that it deserves two entries. The chicken version is served with a clearer and leaner broth.

03 *Bun cha*

Chargrilled pork patties and sliced pork belly served with a herb salad and fresh vermicelli noodles. Try it with *nem cua be* (fried spring rolls with crab).

04 *Bun thang*

A rare, understated and delicate chicken noodle soup, *bun thang* is served with stripped omelette, fresh herbs and shiitake mushrooms.

05 *Bun bo nam bo*

This beef noodle salad is a northern take on a southern favourite, so you might detect a

flavour profile that's a few grades sweeter than most Hanoi dishes.

06 *Banh cuon*

Vietnam's answer to dumplings, these wet rice-paper rolls are light and subtle. They're packed with different fillings depending on the establishment.

07 *Banh tom*

These tantalising little deep-fried dough balls topped with shrimp are favourites of West Lake.

08 *Pho cuon*

A kind of fresh spring roll stuffed with stir-fried beef and served with a sweet-and-sour dipping sauce.

09 *Bia hoi*

A glass of fresh beer is served right on the street and costs less than 50 cents. The best bia hoi joints also serve an unending repertoire of ambitious beer snacks.

03 **PARKS**
& Recreation

**OUTDOORS | ACTIVITY |
PEOPLE-WATCHING**

Hanoi is an assault on the senses, so it's fortuitous that there are several serene pockets in which to unwind when the city gets too overwhelming. In many cases these leafy corners are where communities gather and practise their passions, from hip-hop dance to tai chi, so they also make good spots for people-watching.

🗺 How to

When to go Early in the morning or late in the afternoon if you like the atmosphere of a buzzing outdoor environment. The parks and lakes tend to be quiet at lunchtime.

Opening hours The larger parks open at dawn and close at dusk.

The lakes don't have opening hours.

Chat with locals It's not uncommon for young Vietnamese to approach foreigners to practise their English in parks and around lakes. This is a great way to meet local people, but it's also perfectly acceptable to politely refuse.

HANOI EXPERIENCES

Hoan Kiem Lake & Around

At Hanoi's heart sits Hoan Kiem Lake, a body of water cinematically wrapped by trees and flower gardens. Legend has it that this is where Emperor Le Loi returned the sword he used to protect Vietnam from northern invaders to the turtle god – and that every now and then the deity reveals himself to unsuspecting visitors. It's worth visiting Hoan Kiem Lake several times throughout your stay, whether it's for coffee in the morning, ice cream in the afternoon or a beer in the evening. The lake is especially enjoyable on the weekends when the roads that surround it are traffic-free. Several smaller parks lie within reach of Hoan Kiem Lake, including **Ly Thai To Garden** on P Dinh Tien Hoang, **Hang Trong Garden** on P Nha Chung, and the two triangular parks that flank the **Hanoi Opera House**.

🚶 Early Bird

One of Hanoi's highlights is getting up at the crack of dawn to stroll around Hoan Kiem Lake. You'll see the lakeside activities in full swing, from grannies howling in hysterics during a laughter-yoga session to middle-aged couples dancing passionately to 'La Cumparsita.'

Top left Hoan Kiem Lake **Bottom left** Ly Thai To Garden **Top right** Imperial Citadel (p52)

Thien Quang Lake & Thong Nhat Park

Handsome art-deco houses surround pretty and rarely visited Thien Quang Lake. South of the neighbourhood is Thong Nhat Park, arguably central Hanoi's best spot for an unencumbered walk or jog. There's also an outdoor gym frequented by friendly students who are often keen for a chat, and some fairground rides and jungle gyms that'll keep little ones occupied for an hour or so. The park regularly hosts weekend events like food festivals and book fairs.

The Imperial Citadel & Around

Another large patch of grassland is the Imperial Citadel. There's little to do except marvel at the reconstructed citadel gate, but the tidy lawns and neat pathways make for pleasant, aimless wandering under shady trees. From here you can walk to nearby **Lenin Park**, which is popular with skateboarders and hip-hop dancers, and Ba Dinh Square, which borders the sprawling **Ho Chi Minh Mausoleum Complex**. You'll find street vendors serving

⚑ Banana Island

More of a gigantic green patch of no man's land than a bona fide park, the island in the Song Hong (Red River) known informally as Banana Island is Hanoi's most agrarian neighbourhood. Other than banana plantations, the island supports kumquat tree fields, ostrich pens, a few basic cafes and Hanoi's sole nudist colony! Getting to Banana Island is relatively straightforward: simply walk along Long Bien Bridge and take the steps down to the banana plantations. Once there, walk in any direction you want for as long as you like.

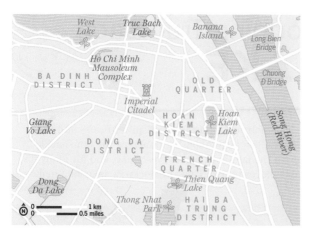

Left Banana Island **Below** Ho Chi Minh Mausoleum & Ba Dinh Square

up traditional sweet snacks in and around both. A little further afield are the **botanical gardens**. There's a small entrance fee, but these majestic gardens are home to frog-filled ponds and some of the city's oldest trees.

West Lake & Around

West Lake is Hanoi's biggest lake by far. A loop of the lake (18km) by bicycle or motorbike, while stopping at pagodas, temples, restaurants and cafes, is an enjoyable way to spend half a day – but watch out for the soul-crushing traffic that consumes the west side of the lake in the early evening. West Lake is also home to three charming peninsular neighbourhoods: Lang Yen Phu, Tu Hoa and Quang An. A **Lang Yen Phu** lakeside cafe makes a good choice to watch the sunset with a coconut, while **Tu Hoa** has a cute collection of artisanal coffee shops and tasty restaurants. **Quang An** is an expat enclave with a plethora of independently run international restaurants and cafes centred around **Quang Ba Garden**. Quang An is worthy of a lazy afternoon or morning lounging around restaurants and cafes, especially when combined with a visit to **Phu Tay Ho**, a stately temple on the shores of the lake.

04 Looping Truc Bach
LAKE

LOCAL FOOD | CAFES & BARS | TEMPLES

▬▬▬ Encircling the little lake of Truc Bach is a mix of spirited cafes and bars, local food and historic sites. The leafy neighbourhood merges the ramshackle charm of the Old Quarter with the laid-back feel of West Lake, and for many it's one of Hanoi's most desirable places to live. This anticlockwise lake loop makes it easy to see why.

🗺 Trip Notes

When to go If it's clear, go in the late afternoon to catch the sunset.

What to bring Comfortable shoes, something to put over your shoulders in the temples, and an appetite.

What next Truc Bach makes a good jumping-off point for further urban adventures. Immediately south is P Phan Dinh Phung, a tree-lined avenue with broad sidewalks and well-preserved French mansions. West Lake to the north is the epicentre of Hanoi's international food scene.

⚒ Bronze Casting

I'm lucky to have been a resident of Truc Bach for eight years, especially as the neighbourhood's secrets kept revealing themselves to me. I remember reading about the area's fascinating bronze-casting history, dating back 500 years. Not long after, I bumped into an ancestor of one of the original casting families. He was one of my neighbours!

■ **Insight from John Kis,** co-founder of Ma Xo cafe @ma.xo.cafe

03 Tran Quoc Pagoda is reportedly Hanoi's oldest Buddhist temple, though rebuilt several times. The towering stupa is an iconic image, especially at sunset.

04 Fresh spring rolls with stir-fried beef (*pho cuon*) is a neighbourhood speciality. There's a row of restaurants serving the dish along Ngu Xa, but the best is **Pho Cuon Chinh Thang**.

West Lake (Ho Tay)

P Nghi Tam

P P Duc

Pho Truc Bach

Ð Yen Phu

05 Close the loop with a drink at **Standing Bar**, a free-house craft-beer pub with dozens of Vietnamese beers and ciders on tap.

Ð Thanh Nien

Truc Bach Lake

Ngu Xa

Ngu Xa

Ngo Tran Vu

P Nguyen Truong

P Quan Thanh

02 Quan Thanh Temple was built 1000 years ago to protect Hanoi from malignant spiritual forces from the north.

P Phan Dinh Phung

01 Start the loop with a coffee (or cocktail) at **Ma Xo**, an artsy streetside cafe that overlooks the lake. You can also ask about any upcoming live music events.

BA DINH DISTRICT

Friendly Fire

BURNING DOWN THE HOUSE

All surviving Vietnamese traditions change with the times, but no custom demonstrates this as fervidly as ancestral worship.

VIETNAM STOCK IMAGES/SHUTTERSTOCK ©

In 2021, when countries were scrambling for COVID-19 vaccines, villages in Vietnam were pumping out thousands of Pfizer jabs. The world hardly took notice of how the manufacturers got their hands on the technology, nor did health officials challenge the vaccines' efficacy and safety. Perhaps it's because the doses are simply cardboard replicas – and they aren't meant for the living.

According to practitioners of joss-paper burning, the ceremonial cremation of diminutive cardboard replicas of everyday essentials, life after death mirrors life before it. They believe these incinerated models will drift into a parallel afterlife and manifest as tangible (and usable) items. Before setting them alight (usually outside the house on the street), the bereaved place the replicas on the family altar and pray to the ancestor that they're for – ensuring the gifts make it to the intended recipient. This can take place decades after the family member's passing, usually on death anniversaries.

The custom has humble beginnings. It started in China centuries ago, but only fake money and gold were burned so that the dead had currency to pay for a comfortable afterlife. Over the years, joss-paper burning has morphed into a more elaborate affair. While money and gold remain the most desirable combustibles, the gift options now include fancy townhouses, dapper clothes, luxury jewellery, air-conditioning units, wi-fi routers, iPhones and more. The surviving family members tend to match the items they purchase with the personalities and passions of the deceased: if grandma was a keen photographer, she receives cameras, lenses and tripods; if grandpa was fond of singing, he's gifted a karaoke machine, microphone and television set.

Left Joss-paper burning **Middle** Tet festivities **Right** Paper house for burning, Hungry Ghost Festival

Despite the custom's ability to adapt and endure, its future remains uncertain. In recent years the local media has looked unfavourably on joss-paper burning, citing environmental and health concerns, and the government occasionally speaks out against overindulgent ancestral-worship practices. Proponents argue that it isn't just cultural heritage, but also a mechanism to cope with loss. The joss-paper-producing villages have entire shops dedicated to children's items, from cardboard cots and prams to paper toys and clothes – a poignant illustration of how some Vietnamese might choose to process the death of a loved one.

> Joss-paper burning isn't just cultural heritage, but also a mechanism to cope with loss.

To get a sense of the custom's diversity, it's best to visit a joss-paper shop. **P Hang Ma**, one of the Old Quarter's most vivid streets, is the traditional place to buy *ma* (joss paper). It has also become the place to go for festival decorations, so you'll have to hunt out the bigger shops that usually keep the cardboard miniatures at the back. Better yet, visit one of the joss-paper-producing villages. **Dao Tu** (p69), 35km west of Hanoi, is the most hectic, with cardboard replicas that spill out onto the street and millions of (fake) dollars packed on the back of motorbikes. **Phuc Am**, 17km south of Hanoi, is a quieter village specialising in joss-paper models to commemorate national heroes during elaborate ceremonies. Multicoloured horses, glistening dragons, gigantic boats and armoured platoons fill the workhouses.

☼ When to See It

Death anniversaries Death anniversary ceremonies occur on the date the deceased passed away, so they may happen at any time during the year.

Vietnamese New Year (Tet) The days preceding and following Vietnam's biggest holiday, which falls in January or February, can be particularly incendiary.

Hungry Ghost Festival This spirited festival is when the gates of hell are thrown open, enabling wraiths to roam the land of the living. It begins on the 15th day of the seventh lunar month (usually August or September). People often burn joss paper to satisfy these vacationing spirits – and to keep them from wreaking havoc.

05 Medley of MUSEUMS

MUSEUMS | CULTURE | HISTORY

Hanoi is Vietnam's cultural and political hub, so it should come as no surprise that it's also home to the country's best museums. But choose carefully: it's usually better to invest more time in the museums that really appeal than trying to tick off all the boxes.

How to

When to go Most museums in Hanoi are open every day, including Mondays, but always check online first. Note that some may close at lunchtime.

Guide or no guide As a general rule, a guide is essential for the National Museum of Vietnamese History and the Fine Arts Museum, where the displays are interesting but the information poor. You can make do in the others without one, though a guide will always help get under the skin of the content.

For history buffs Housed in a huge colonial building that blends European and Asian aesthetics, the **National Museum of Vietnamese History** is worth visiting for the architecture alone. If you venture inside, you'll discover dusty – but not uninteresting – displays that cover Vietnam's history from the Dong Son culture (3rd century BCE to 3rd century CE) up until the revolutionary movement in 1945. The building that houses the **Fine Arts Museum** is less remarkable, but the artworks tell enthralling stories, from France's lasting impact on Vietnam's

Map labels:
0 1 km
0 0.5 miles
West Lake (Ho Tay)
Truc Bach Lake
Song Hong (Red River)
Long Bien Bridge
BA DINH DISTRICT
Chuong D Bridge
OLD QUARTER
Ho Chi Minh Museum
Fine Arts Museum
HOAN KIEM DISTRICT
National Museum of Vietnamese History
DONG DA DISTRICT
Vietnamese Women's Museum
FRENCH QUARTER
Vietnam Museum of Ethnology (4.2km); Press Museum (Dinh Nghe) (5.6km)
Thong Nhat Park
Bay Mau Lake
HAI BA TRUNG DISTRICT

Top right Vietnam Museum of Ethnology **Bottom right** National Museum of Vietnamese History

HANOI EXPERIENCES

📖 Read All About It

Given Vietnam's appalling record for press freedoms (175th out of 180 countries – worse than Cuba, Syria and Iran – according to Reporters Without Borders in 2021), Hanoi's strangest museum might be the **Press Museum (Dinh Nghe)**, which opened in 2020. Prepare for plenty of propaganda.

creative scene to how art was – and is – harnessed for propagandist purposes. **For culture vultures** The **Vietnam Museum of Ethnology** is one of the country's standout museums, detailing the history and culture of Vietnam's diverse ethnic tapestry. A highlight is the back garden, with a collection of traditional structures built by the different ethnic groups. The highly informative **Vietnamese Women's Museum** sensitively explores the country's history and culture from the female perspective, including the role of women during the wars and the hardship experienced by Hanoi's street hawkers. The expansive, Soviet-style **Ho Chi Minh Museum** explores the illustrious life of modern Vietnam's founding father while offering an insight into his impact on contemporary life.

06 Cocktail-Bar **CRAWL**

NIGHTLIFE | COCKTAILS | MUSIC

The Old Quarter's convoluted road network and parasitic architecture have hatched secret speakeasies buried down alleyways and kooky cocktail bars resting above storefronts. When you've had enough of squatting on the pavement and chugging *bia hoi* (as fun as that is), try this eclectic cocktail-bar crawl.

The *Pho* Cocktail

The story behind the *pho* cocktail is reflected in history. Hanoi was bombed relentlessly during the war, so I designed the cocktail preparation to look like bombs falling. Liquid is set alight and then cascades from tiered metal compartments before making its way to the glass. At the same time, it draws on Hanoi cuisine's unique flavour profile.

■ Insight from **Pham Tien Tiep,** *co-founder of Ne Cocktail Bar @nehanoi*

🗺 Trip Notes

When to go Any time after 6pm. Message ahead on Facebook or Instagram to book a table (and find out if there's live music).

What to wear Anything you like, though you'll feel out of place in flip-flops and a vest top.

How to get around This itinerary features two pockets of cocktail bars: Bee'Znees and Ne Cocktail Bar to the east of Hoan Kiem Lake, and the rest to the west. Consider taking a taxi between these two clusters.

02 Continue the crawl in **Bee'Znees**, a Roaring Twenties–inspired speakeasy concealed behind a pretend bookshop. You'll need to pull the right book to open the bookcase. Hint: 'Hello old sport!'

03 Leo's is a swanky city cocktail bar with on-point mood lighting, theatrical mixology and a seasonal cocktail menu. Or just tell the English-speaking bartenders what you fancy.

01 Ne Cocktail Bar was co-founded by the creator of the *pho* cocktail, which uses the same herbs and spices as Vietnam's world-famous dish. It would be a crime to order anything else.

05 Kumquat Tree morphs from cocktail bar to miniature nightclub with regular DJ nights past midnight, so it's the perfect bar to keep the party going.

04 Established by journalist, aesthete and raconteur Nguyen Qui Duc, **Tadioto** has become something of a Hanoi institution. Peruse the wine list if you're winding down for the evening.

OLD QUARTER

HOAN KIEM DISTRICT

Hoan Kiem Lake

HAI BA TRUNG DISTRICT

0   200 m
0   0.1 miles

D Tran Nhat Duat

Song Hong (Red River)

P Hang Dieu
P Hang Non
P Hang Quat
P Luong Van Can
P Cau Go
P Nguyen Huu Huan
P Hang Gai
Lo Su
D Tran Quang Khai
P Hang Ga
P Ly Thai To
Tong Duy Tan
P Phung Hung
P Hang Bong
P Ngo Quyen
P Tong Dan
P Le Thai To
P Dinh Tien Hoang
P Le Thanh Tong
P Trang Thi
P Hang Khay
P Trang Tien
P Nguyen Khac Can
P Ngo Quyen

ARCHITECTURE
Through the Ages

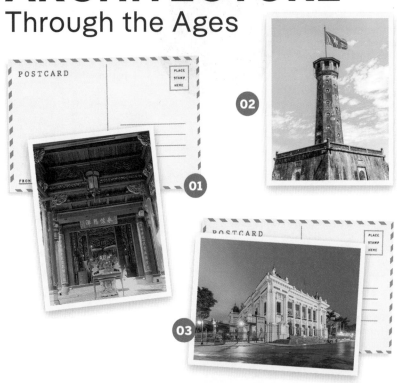

01 Bach Ma Temple

Dating from the 11th century, this is debatably Hanoi's oldest temple though most of the current structure only dates back a few hundred years.

02 Flag Tower

The handsome, hexagonal and climbable Flag Tower is Hanoi's iconic piece of architecture from the Nguyen dynasty era (19th century).

03 Hanoi Opera House

This flamboyant, ostentatious opera house was modelled on Paris' Palais Garnier in the 1900s, reflecting France's desires to fashion a colony in its own image.

04 State Bank of Vietnam

In the 1930s, towards the end of the French colonial period, art deco was gaining in popularity, as evidenced by the angularity of the State Bank building.

05 Hanoi Train Station

Bombed during the American War, the central hall was rebuilt in the 1970s with a commanding mashrabiya facade, a popular architectural cooling technique of reunified Vietnam.

06 Ho Chi Minh Museum

Whether you love it or hate it, the Ho Chi Minh Museum building – dating from the 1990s and adorned with eye-catching communist imagery – never fails to make an impression.

07 Lotte Center Hanoi

A symbol of Hanoi's modern aspirations, the glass-coated Lotte Center Hanoi from the 2010s is one of the tallest buildings in Vietnam. The 65th-floor Observation Deck affords unrivalled views.

07 Open-Air
ART

STREET ART | OUTDOORS | WALKING

Hanoi is a rabbit warren of alleyways that carve up a mishmash of architectural styles. Among this perplexity you'll find some of Southeast Asia's most fanciful urban art, from awe-inspiring murals to eye-catching graffiti. These pockets of creativity make for heartening strolls while discovering the capital, and it's worth going well out of your way for some.

🗺 How to

Guide or no guide?
When there is information, it's scarce, but there's no need to engage a guide for Hanoi's open-air art.

How to visit Simply find the neighbourhood and wander at will. Many spots are close to or on the way to sights and museums, so you can map out your day to include them in your itinerary.

When to go Any time during the day.

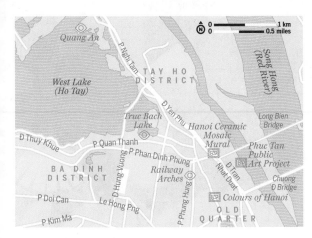

Top & bottom left Hanoi Ceramic Mosaic Mural

The **Hanoi Ceramic Mosaic Mural**, which celebrates the city's millennial anniversary, is long enough to traverse four streets: Tran Nhat Duat, Yen Phu, Nghi Tam and Au Co. As it lines a busy roadway, the mosaic wall is better appreciated inside a car or on a motorbike taxi rather than on foot. Mosaic depictions include the iconic sites of Hanoi, areas of natural beauty in Vietnam and the ancient cities of Southeast Asia.

In the Old Quarter, the **Colours of Hanoi** was commissioned to liven up the ubiquitous sidewalk electricity boxes. It's the kind of art you might miss unless you know what to look for: keep an eye out for paintings of peach blossoms, kumquat trees and other native Vietnamese flora. In the same neighbourhood are the 100-year-old **railway arches** which, at the northern end of Phung Hung, have been filled in and painted with illusory trompe-l'oeil scenes of Hanoi life over the decades. The arches have since become a popular selfie spot for locals.

A little further to the north are Truc Bach and West Lake, two more pockets with outdoor art worth hunting out. On **Truc Bach Lake**, the houses overlooking the water and next to the park have been painted with images to encourage conscientious urban living. The **Quang An** neighbourhood in West Lake is also dotted with ambitious and compelling murals, such as the engrossing faces by muralist Nah Mate, who has been giving character to streets in Southeast Asia since 2016.

Phuc Tan Public Art Project

Hanoi's most extraordinary outdoor art project hides in a ramshackle neighbourhood behind Long Bien Market, Hanoi's oldest and biggest. To show that art can live alongside any community, Nguyen The Son, an artist and lecturer at the Vietnam Fine Arts University, gathered local and international creatives and embarked on an ambitious project like no other. Images of boats sail on waves made of recycled plastic bottles, a multicoloured dragon made from broken glass meanders along the wall, and displays of feudal life are embossed on large sheets of metal. The installations are just south of Long Bien Bridge on the last street before the river.

66

08 Craft
ATTACK

SHOPPING | CRAFTS | VILLAGES

Hanoi has spent much of its 1000-year history as the seat of ruling dynasties. Over the centuries, rural villages adopted (or were assigned) a craft – from conical hats to coffins – to supply for the Hanoi elite. Some of these villages make for compelling day trips.

Top left Conical hat weavers, Chuong (p68) **Bottom right** Woman wearing an *ao dai* (p68) **Top right** Traditional artists, Hanoi

🗺 How to

Getting around Most craft villages are about an hour by car or motorbike from Hanoi, as well as at least an hour from each other. When planning your itinerary, consider their geographical proximity.

When to go Any day at any time of year

(the artisans also work weekends).

What time In many villages, activity happens in the morning (7am to 10am) and the afternoon (3pm to 6pm). If you're making a day of it, leave early, take a leisurely lunch break and expect to be back after dark.

Escape to the Countryside

Hanoi's surrounding craft villages number in the hundreds. In some, the villagers have given up on the craft and sought more lucrative professions. In others, gigantic factories continue the craft culture but have bulldozed the charm of family ateliers. However, a collection of pretty villages where families continue to transfer their skills and knowledge still exist, and these are the ones that are most worthy of a visit. The artisans receive very little interest or attention, and they are usually keen to demonstrate their skills to curious visitors.

Food Culture

Cooking and food is an intrinsic part of Vietnam's culture, and some villages took it upon themselves to specialise in crafting ingredients, from noodles and rice crackers to

🍃 Support the Crafts

Hanoi's craft villages provide thousands of jobs in rural parts of the country. Visiting the villages, meeting the families, learning about the history and perhaps buying some souvenirs is not just a way of keeping the craft culture going; it also helps support people's livelihoods.

■ **Recommended by Tran Thuy Hai,** *Hanoi-based travel consultant and sustainable-tourism specialist* @tranthuyhai

tofu and soya milk. South of Hanoi sits **Cu Da**, which specialises in glass-noodle production. This is one of Hanoi's most photogenic villages, as enormous bunches of yellow and white translucent noodles hang from canopies to dry before being packed on motorbikes and shipped off to the city. North of Hanoi in Bac Ninh province lies **Tho Ha**, which used to specialise in pottery but now focuses on rice paper. If you visit on a dry day, you'll find drying racks for rice paper on almost every horizontal surface, including balconies, rooftops, alleyways and parks.

Iconic Clothing

Vietnam's two most recognisable items of clothing are *ao dai* (long tunic) and *non* (conical hat). **Van Phuc**, southwest of Hanoi, is the silk village where you'll find good-value scarves, ties and shirts, as well as rows of dazzling *ao dai*. West of Hanoi in Ha Tay province, **Chuong** is one of the prettiest villages, with an intact entrance gate, lots of trees

Bat Trang Craft Village

A little over half an hour from the Old Quarter by motorised transport, centuries-old Bat Trang is Hanoi's most frequently visited craft village – and with good reason. The pottery village is packed with shops and market clusters selling high-quality and reasonably priced crockery that's fired in Bat Trang's various kilns (some of which are visitable historical relics). A rabbit warren of alleyways separates the shops from the river and is well worth getting lost in, as is the **Bat Trang Museum**, housed in a contemporary structure inspired by the village's heritage.

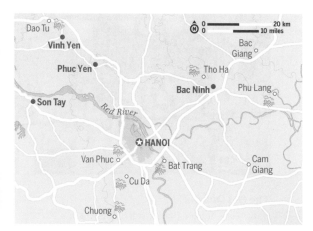

Left Pottery, Bat Trang **Below** Coffins, Phu Lang

and several canals and ponds. While wandering around, you can peer into family homes to see people weaving the conical hats for which the village is famous.

Death & the Afterlife

Dying (and the journey thereafter) is somewhat of an obsession in Vietnam, with some families contributing eye-watering amounts of money to funerals, tombs and ceremonies for the deceased. This preoccupation is reflected in a couple of craft villages. **Dao Tu**, west of Hanoi, is one of the best places to see joss-paper models of money, houses, mod-cons and other must-haves for the dead. These items are ceremoniously burned before wafting into the afterlife and reappearing as real and usable objects (p56). Northeast of Hanoi in Bac Ninh province, **Phu Lang** is a pottery village that specialises in coffins. Those that pass the test are shipped off to funeral parlours across northern Vietnam, but the duds stay back to be used for construction. As you walk around the small streets of the village, you'll notice that many of the walls are built from crooked coffins.

(Window) Shopper's Paradise

SPECIAL FINDS FOR ALL BUDGETS

An ancient trading quarter, bulging markets, a resilient art scene and a budding urban youth culture combine to craft Vietnam's most multifarious shopping opportunities.

TRONG NGUYEN/SHUTTERSTOCK ©

The Old Quarter

Hanoi's labyrinthine Old Quarter has been a hub of trade and commerce for over a thousand years, as evidenced by the descriptive street names. Hang means 'product' in Vietnamese, and P Hang Bac, P Hang Thiec and Hang Tre refer to silver, tin and bamboo products, respectively. Most streets no longer sell the products they're named after, but some do.

Streets of particular interest to bric-a-brac hunters are **P To Tich**, which sells puppets; **P Hang Quat**, which sells religious and funeral trinkets; and **P Thuoc Bac**, which sells traditional medicine. The square block encompassing **P Hang Trong**, **P Ly Quoc Su**, **P Hang Gai** and **P Nha Tho** has some excellent, unusual boutiques peddling fashionable clothes, artisanal souvenirs and fabrics from the minority people of the northern mountains.

There are, of course, bargains to be had in the Old Quarter, though quality can be questionable. Bargaining is permissible if there isn't a price tag, but check similar items in other shops first: traders in Hanoi won't appreciate being offered less than the item's value.

Markets

Unpacking Hanoi's myriad markets is well worth the effort, even if you don't end up making a purchase. **Long Bien food market**, **Chau Long food market** and **Quang Ba flower market** are best just before sunrise. Multicoloured **Hom fabric market** makes for excellent photo opportunities, while the gigantic and centrally located **Dong Xuan market** sells practically everything, though quality can vary.

Left Shopfront, P Hang Trong
Middle Long Bien food market
Right Kilomet 109 design

Art

Despite the government's ambivalent attitude to artistic freedoms, Hanoi remains an excellent place to buy art. **Thang Long Art Gallery**, **Green Palm Art Gallery** and **Nguyen Art Gallery** all have excellent reputations and display a range of work from established local artists. All the work is for sale, but the salespeople aren't pushy – they'll let you wander around even if you have no intention of buying.

> Unpacking Hanoi's myriad markets is well worth the effort, even if you don't end up making a purchase.

Forever Young

Hanoi's younger generations are behind an assortment of boutique shops worth hunting out. **Hien Van Ceramics** is packed with handcrafted ceramic products, from vases modelled on distillation jars to ornamental animals. **Vui Studio** designs and produces all its crafts in house; expect a broad selection, including soaps, bags and cushion covers. **Zo Paper** specialises in artisanal paper products, while **aN Store** concentrates on leather. One of Hanoi's most interesting shops is **Tired City**, which has hip designs from prominent local artists printed on T-shirts, posters, playing cards and more. 'We found tonnes of potential artwork created by local young artists, most of which was just lying silently in their sketchbooks or laptops', says Nguyen Viet Nam, its founder and director. 'We felt the urge to dig it up and put it on display.'

☵ Waterside Fashion

Three of Hanoi's best fashion boutiques overlook the tranquil West Lake waters.

Kilomet 109 A visionary designer and fierce proponent of slow fashion, Thao Vu set up the award-winning Kilomet 109 to support local artisans and help preserve traditional techniques.

Gian Don This shop has a healthy selection of tasteful linen products in muted tones.

Chula Weaving Vietnamese patterns with Spanish flair, Catalan couple Laura Fontan and Diego Cortizas offer a daring line-up of eye-catching attire.

Listings

BEST OF THE REST

 Unique Eats

Tung Dining $$$

Arguably Hanoi's most interesting restaurant, award-winning Tung Dining offers exceptional fine dining in the Old Quarter, with only one set menu that guides you through a series of around 20 expertly prepared dishes. Definite splurge opportunity. Bookings essential.

Nha Hang Tam Vi $$

Tam Vi serves up traditional northern fare in quaint surroundings on the road connecting the Temple of Literature with the Old Quarter. There's an elegant picture menu that makes for easy ordering, and the tofu dishes are particularly good.

Masu $$$

Another splurge option, especially if you'd like to refresh your palate after a deluge of Vietnamese food. Masu offers contemporary Japanese cuisine in Hanoi's stately French Quarter. It rivals anything you'll find in Tokyo.

Pho Ly Van Phuc $

'Chicken Street' is a grilled-meat enclave that divides opinion, and there's no denying that the sweet aroma of the outdoor grills will tempt the taste buds. Proponents speak about rock-bottom prices and an unbeatable atmosphere; haters reference the question-able hygiene standards of some vendors.

Ngoam $$

Don't be surprised if you go away wondering if this is the best burger you've ever eaten. Ngoam's creative menu boasts mouth-watering burgers with add-ons like miso aioli and fermented sticky rice; it's close to St Joseph Cathedral.

Uu Dam Chay $$

An indulgent vegan restaurant spread over multiple floors in the French Quarter, Uu Dam Chay is surprisingly affordable given the glitzy clientele. Reservations advisable.

Vua Cha Ca $$

There are a couple of these *cha ca* (fried fish) restaurants dotted around Hanoi. It's a must-try dish, especially as it's almost impossible to find outside the capital, and this modern, family-friendly restaurant is one of the better ones on offer. Bookings advisable.

Paperman $

Paperman serves reliably good takeaway *banh mi* (Vietnamese baguette). Take the sandwich around the corner and sit at one of the *tra chanh da* (iced lemon tea) stalls while you gaze at St Joseph Cathedral.

 Draught Beer

P Ta Hien $

A *bia hoi* (draught beer) on P Ta Hien is somewhat of a rite of passage. The dirt-cheap prices attract tourists and locals alike, and the people-watching is second to none.

John McCain Monument

Bia Hai Xom $$

There are a handful of Bia Hai Xom restaurants in central Hanoi serving up reliably good fare to pair with their ice-cold beer in basic surroundings.

Quan Bia Hoi Bat Dan $

Smack-bang in the centre of the Old Quarter is this friendly beer joint. The clientele is rowdy but friendly, and the staff will do their best to help you decode the Vietnamese menu.

Uncanny War Sights

John McCain Monument

John McCain was shot down over Truc Bach Lake in the 1960s and then dragged from the muddy waters by locals. A monument stands on Đ Thanh Nien to mark the event.

B52 Lake

In the 1970s a B52, an American strategic bomber, crash-landed in Hanoi. Part of the wreckage was left in a lake in Ba Dinh to serve as a poignant reminder.

Long Bien Bridge

One of Hanoi's iconic landmarks, Long Bien Bridge was bombed so aggressively during the American War that it's a miracle it's still standing.

Live Music & Performances

Hanoi Opera House

The grand Hanoi Opera House has an eclectic performance schedule, hosting international dance troupes, flamboyant musicals and classical music.

Binh Minh Jazz Club

Hanoi's first jazz club is still its best, with nightly performances starting at around 8pm. The line-up is always slightly different, so feel free to visit more than once. It's behind the Opera House.

Performers, Hanoi Opera House

R&R

Yakushi Center

A favourite with expats and locals alike, Yakushi Center in Tay Ho offers reliable and good-value massages in a no-frills setting. Rooms are shared, but the curtain dividers provide plenty of privacy. Tipping not required.

Dao's Care

This charming social enterprise offers treatments inspired by the ethnic minority people in Vietnam's northern mountains. Consider a therapeutic Dao bath made with foraged medicinal herbs. Tipping optional.

Huong Sen

Traditional Vietnamese spa experiences tend to be more structured than Western ones. At Huong Sen, you'll move through steam rooms, herbal Jacuzzis and cold saunas before finishing with a massage. Tipping the massage therapist is essential.

Scan to find more things to do in Hanoi online

NHAC NGUYEN/GETTY IMAGES ©

NORTHERN VIETNAM

ADVENTURE | NATURE | ETHNIC GROUPS

Experience Northern Vietnam online

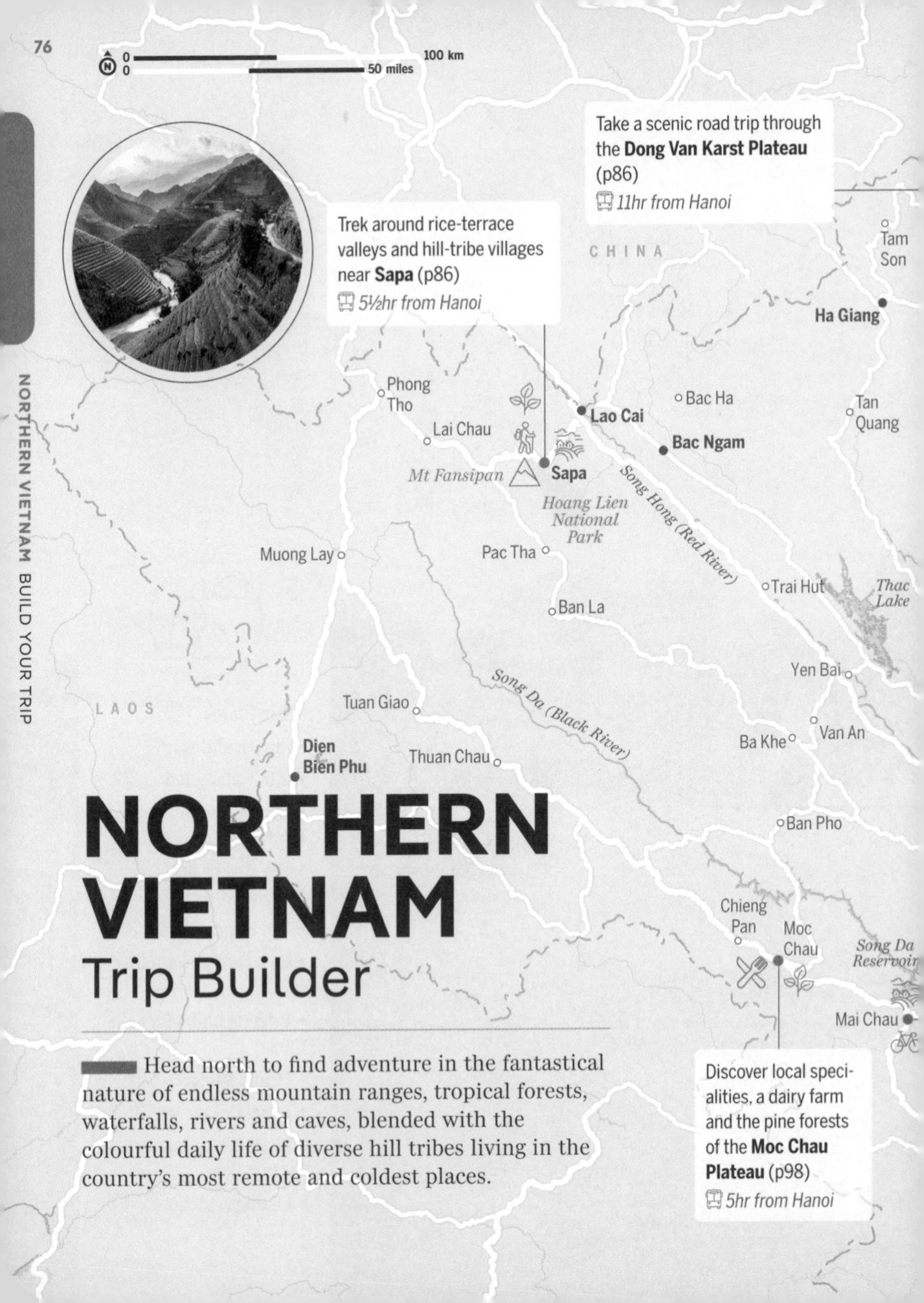

N

0 ——— 0 ——— 100 km
50 miles

Take a scenic road trip through the **Dong Van Karst Plateau** (p86)
🚌 *11hr from Hanoi*

Trek around rice-terrace valleys and hill-tribe villages near **Sapa** (p86)
🚌 *5½hr from Hanoi*

CHINA

Tam Son

Ha Giang

Phong Tho

Bac Ha

Tan Quang

Lai Chau

Lao Cai

Bac Ngam

Mt Fansipan **Sapa**

Hoang Lien National Park

Song Hong (Red River)

Muong Lay

Pac Tha

Trai Hut

Thac Lake

Ban La

Yen Bai

L A O S

Song Da (Black River)

Tuan Giao

Ba Khe

Van An

Dien Bien Phu

Thuan Chau

Ban Pho

NORTHERN VIETNAM
Trip Builder

Chieng Pan

Moc Chau

Song Da Reservoir

Mai Chau

Head north to find adventure in the fantastical nature of endless mountain ranges, tropical forests, waterfalls, rivers and caves, blended with the colourful daily life of diverse hill tribes living in the country's most remote and coldest places.

Discover local specialities, a dairy farm and the pine forests of the **Moc Chau Plateau** (p98)
🚌 *5hr from Hanoi*

CHINA
Dong Van
Na Phong
Cao Bang
Quang Uyen
Na Loung
Na Phac
Ba Be National Park
Bac Kan
Bac Son
Lang Son
Tuyen Quang
Bien Dong
Bac Giang
Tien Yen
Mong Cai
Viet Tri
Vinh Yen
HANOI
Halong City
Cam Pha
Bai Tu Long Bay
Hoa Binh
Haiphong
Gulf of Tonkin
Phu Nho Quan
Nam Dinh
Thai Binh
Ninh Binh
Cam Thuy

Hike or take a boat tour on the lake in **Ba Be National Park** (p92)
4½hr from Hanoi

Go on a cruise amid the karst scenery of **Halong Bay** (p80)
3hr from Hanoi

Hike in the year-round temperate climate of **Tam Dao National Park** (p101)
1½hr from Hanoi

Cycle to villages and sleep in stilt houses in **Mai Chau** (p91)
2½hr from Hanoi

Sunbathe, cycle or hike on green **Cat Ba Island** (p101)
\+ *1½hr from Hai Phong*

Explore bookable experiences in Northern Vietnam

FROM LEFT: BJORN PROFESSIONAL/SHUTTERSTOCK © GALYNA ANDRUSHKO/SHUTTERSTOCK © NGUYEN QUANG NGOC TONKIN/SHUTTERSTOCK © PREVIOUS SPREAD: JUNPHOTO/SHUTTERSTOCK ©

Practicalities

VIETNAM STOCK PHOTOS/SHUTTERSTOCK ©

ARRIVING

Noi Bai International Airport, Hanoi Budget flights are available to domestic airports of Van Don (Quang Ninh province) and Cat Bi (Hai Phong province).

Hanoi Train Station connects many routes to popular destinations in various provinces.

Hanoi's bus stations The three largest ones – My Dinh, Gia Lam and Yen Nghia – are linked directly with most places in the region.

HOW MUCH FOR A

**cup of coffee
15,000d**

**bowl of *pho*
20,000d**

**brocade souvenir
from 50,000d**

GETTING AROUND

Motorbike Renting a motorbike is the easiest and fastest way to get around the mountainous areas with dirt roads and slopes. Rental shops are found in city and town centres; prices range from 100,000d to 150,000d per day.

Motorbike taxi Some local drivers offer their services if you want a motorbike riding experience but don't want to drive yourself. The cost depends on the schedule and destinations, starting from 100,000d one way and 150,000d for a round trip.

Cycling or walking If your schedule is flexible and you have time, this is a good way to get around.

WHEN TO GO

JAN–MAR
Cold, rainy and wet, with beautiful spring blossoms.

APR–JUN
Fine and settled weather, perfect for outdoor adventure.

JUL–SEP
Hot and stuffy; good for islands, beaches and boat trips.

OCT–DEC
Fine and settled weather, perfect for outdoor adventure.

EATING & DRINKING

The *lon cap nach* (little black pig), naturally bred in the mountains and forests, provides the favourite food of the northern region, prepared as various steamed, stirred, grilled and soup dishes. Popular street BBQ, either roadside or in local markets, comes with diverse fresh products that are home-grown and bred on the fields and in the forests. Two of the most common drinks among the people of the northern mountains, especially in winter, are corn and *tao meo* (wild edible fruit) wine.

Best black pig A Phu Restaurant, Sapa (p99)

Must-try BBQ Chicken mixed with fruit spice at local markets

CONNECT & FIND YOUR WAY

Wi-fi Available at most cafes, bars and restaurants if you order a cup of coffee or something else.

Navigation Difficult in small towns and villages as there are usually no addresses or street numbers. Stay connected and use the navigation apps on your phone. Offline Mapme is a useful one.

MONEY

Carry cash – dong, always including some small notes. Many small shops are very cheap and don't even have change for big notes. Most places don't accept foreign currency or cards.

WHERE TO STAY

Thanks to the diverse topography of mountains, forests, rivers, delta and sea, the north provides various distinctive accommodation options in all price ranges.

City/Town	Pro/Con
Halong City	Cruises or junk boats in Halong Bay for sunset and night views. More costly than average hotels, starting from 2,500,000d per cabin.
Sapa	Hill resorts, ecolodges or guesthouses with rooftops looking across terrace fields. Usually not in town centre.
Mai Chau	Traditional stilt houses of local people in villages surrounded by mountains, gardens and fields. Possible lack of privacy as everyone sleeps in the same place.
Ha Giang	Homestays with homemade food and drinks.

VILLAGE TABOOS

Don't enter a village if there's a tree branch or bamboo fence with some ox bones at the entrance – it signals that ritual ceremonies are taking place and strangers aren't welcome.

09 Into Halong BAY

ADVENTURE | OUTDOORS | SPORTS

▬▬▬ Whether it's splashing below or above the water, or climbing to the top of islets scattered about, you'll find plenty of activities at the World Heritage Site of Halong Bay and fictional home of King Kong. Explore this tropical oceanic ecosystem where limestone mountains over 500 million years old rise above the sea.

LENA SERDITOVA/SHUTTERSTOCK ©

🗺 How to

Getting here Frequent daily buses run from Hanoi's My Dinh, Giap Bat or Gia Lam stations to Halong City, where you can take a boat trip.

When to go April to June and September to November is the best weather. Avoid rainy July and August, busy weekends and public holidays.

Tour cost From 500,000d per person including admission, food and some activities – more economical than only a regular boat ticket (150,000d to 250,000d per person).

POCHOLO T CALAPRE/SHUTTERSTOCK ©

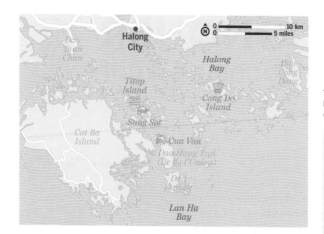

Top left Kayakers, Halong Bay
Bottom left Tai chi, Halong Bay boat cruise

Kayaking Kayak over the tranquil water for both fun and freedom: get closer to unnamed green islets, pass natural limestone archways and mysterious caves, discover lagoons and deserted beaches, or observe the peaceful life of floating fishing villages.

Swimming Take a dip in the cool water and sunbathe on smooth white-sand beaches with views of karst mountains all around.

Climbing The rocky mountains on the islands, which come in various shapes (cliffs, chimneys, dihedrals, slopes), provide a new challenge even for professional climbers. The prize is at the top: views across the bay from high above, stunning at sunrise.

Snorkelling Scuba dive or snorkel to discover the bay's colourful 'water gardens' of a hundred coral-reef species across dozens of hectares. They are concentrated in the areas of **Cong Do Island**, **Van Gio Island** and **Trai Cave**.

Squid-hunting Join local fishers to learn about a part of their life and enjoy the tranquil night views of the bay as well as your fresh 'trophy' – delicious squid dishes, one of the specialities from Halong Bay.

Overnight cruising Spending a night on a cruise or a junk boat provides night views of the bay, totally different from the daytime journey: watch as the sun gradually goes down over the sea and the stars appear. Tai chi and yoga at sunrise will recharge you with new energy to start the day.

Best Spots in the Bay

Caves One of Halong Bay's treasures, formed millions of years ago with many stalactites and stalagmites in various shapes and sizes. The most popular caves are **Sung Sot** (Surprise), **Dau Go** (Wooden Stakes), **Thien Cung** (Heaven), **Sang Toi** (Dark and Light) and **Me Cung** (Maze).

Floating villages Villages like **Cua Van**, **Ba Hang** or **Vung Vieng**, home to many local people, portray the simple and happy life of these communities on the sea.

Titop Island This island boasts the wild beauty of plants, trees and wildlife. While the crescent-moon-shaped beach is fun for playing in the water, the 100m-high mountain is tempting for hiking and a nice view from the top.

■ Recommend by Pham Ha, *CEO of Luxury Travel DMC @heritagecruises*

10 CONQUER
Indochina's Roof

CLIMBING | MOUNTAIN | ADVENTURE

▬▬▬ Summiting Fansipan (3143m), the highest mountain in Indochina, is the dream of all local climbers, trekkers and fans of mountains and adventure. The journey provides not only the challenges of rough dirt roads, cliffs and slopes, but also the natural beauty of Hoang Lien National Park with thousands of plant species, including some rare ones only found here.

🗺 How to

Getting here Fansipan is only about 9km from the centre of Sapa. Trains and buses from Hanoi to Sapa run daily.

When to go October to December is the best weather, and March is the rhododendron blooming time. Avoid the rainy season from May to September.

Hire a local porter They guide the route, carry your stuff and prepare food for you (about 400,000d per day for four people).

Choose Your Route

Tram Ton Pass Starting at the height of 1900m, thanks to its smooth road, the most comfortable and popular route is suitable for beginners and those with an average level of fitness alike. It takes two days and one night but very fit hikers can do it in one day.

Sin Chai village Beginning at 1260m, this is the shortest route with many high slopes, ideal for those who are quite fit and tight for time. It features a nice landscape, including a bamboo forest. It takes two days or longer.

Cat Cat village Taking off from 1245m, the longest

Top right Dancers, Fansipan Legend **Bottom right** Cable car, Fansipan

❄ Fansipan Festivals

Khen Festival The region's largest pan-pipe competition, in January and February.

Rhododendron Festival Held from March to May, during the blooming season.

Food Festival July and August showcase regional dishes, with cooking contests, folk games and dances.

Winter Festival In December, European Christmas atmosphere meets Vietnam's mountainous spirit.

and most challenging route has dangerous cliffs and slopes, requiring climbers to sometimes use ropes or other special facilities. But it's the most interesting road for experienced climbers. with diverse scenery from the beginning to the end of the trip. The usual schedule for this route is three to four days.

Cable car Located in the **Fansipan Legend** tourist area, 3km away from central Sapa, it will take you to Fansipan peak in only 15 minutes, instead of a few days. It's also a good way to contemplate the views across the Muong Hoa Valley and Hoang Lien National Park from an altitude of thousands of metres.

■ **Additional insights from Linh Cecilia,** *a blogger with a passion for mountain climbing @linhh.lia*

The Call of the
NORTHWEST

NATURE | ADVENTURE | CULTURE

Intrepid travellers will find it hard to resist the call of Vietnam's northwest. The perfect way to explore the region's spectacular scenery is on a road trip that takes you along zigzagging mountain passes, past golden terrace fields and through ethnic-minority villages – whether you choose to hike or travel by motorcycle.

How to

Getting around Motorbike, bicycle or hiking is the best way. Rental shops are found in the centre of main towns.

When to go All year round; each season has its own beauty.

Road-trip essentials Bring rain gear, basic medications, some dried food and a local SIM card. Pharmacies, convenience stores and restaurants are not always available. Petrol stations are much less frequent on the minor roads, so stock up on fuel.

Nature Thrills

Mountain kingdom Immerse yourself in the sublime highland scenery of lush tropical forests, misty peaks, winding roads, patchworks of yellow rice-terrace fields during harvest season, and hill-tribe villages scattered in remote valleys.

Downhill slopes Zigzagging mountain passes are both a challenge and a pleasure for drivers. Going downhill, with mountain views on one side and the abyss on the other, can be a 'fast and furious' kind of thrill. Make sure to control the speed, keep your eyes on the road and avoid driving at night.

The Open Road

New roads With the convenience of your own vehicle and especially if your schedule is flexible, there are usually various routes

Most Challenging Mountain Passes

Ma Pi Leng The country's most dangerous and spectacular road, with many steep slopes and the striking canyon of Nho Que River.

O Quy Ho The longest pass stretches for 50km at the highest altitude of 2000m above sea level, covered by clouds all year round.

Top left Ma Pi Leng pass **Bottom left** O Quy Ho **Top right** Village life, northwest Vietnam

to get to a destination and many chances to pick one spontaneously, without planning – simply because it seems to hide something interesting and you're eager to see where it leads you.

Hidden destinations The road may take you to a gorgeous valley, a fresh stream, a beautiful garden filled with fruits, traditional houses and fences made of rocks, or a tranquil field of cows grazing the grass.

Roadside food Along the way you may also follow delicious smells, and come across small food stalls with dishes ranging from simple grilled corn and sweet potatoes to hot rice soup, pancakes, five-colour sticky rice or BBQ.

Cultural Exchanges

Making friends In the countryside, it's easy to catch local people on their way to work and groups of kids walking back from school or just playing around their homes – they will

◎ Best of the Northwest

Harvest season In September and October, the rice terrace fields in **Sapa**, **Mu Cang Chai** and **Hoang Su Phi** turn golden yellow. In May and June, water turns the paddies into giant mirrors.

Sea of clouds Rise above the clouds from November to March on peaks above 2000m, at **Y Ty** (Lao Cai province), **Ta Xua** (Son La province), **Sin Ho** (Lai Chau province) or **Ta Chi Nhua** (Yen Bai province).

Blossom seasons The region's colours include white and pink from plum and peach blossoms in January and February, white from orchid trees in March, red from rhododendron in April, purple pink from buckwheat in November, and yellow from rapeseed in December.

Dong Van Karst Plateau The country's most magnificent karst mountains: steep cliffs, deep canyons, serene valleys and twisting roads.

Far left Dong Van Karst Plateau **Near left** Stilt house, Sapa Valley **Below** Rice terraces, Mu Cang Chai

usually wave and say 'Hello' *(xin chao)* to travellers. With a bit of luck, if you visit during a holiday or a festival (and there are many throughout the year), you will get invited to join in the festive atmosphere and try special food and drinks. Remember to say a firm 'No' *(khong)* to offers of shots if you don't want to drink more; otherwise you risk not remembering anything else until you wake up the next day, thanks to the traditional local hospitality.

Varied stays Hotels and guesthouses are found at all popular destinations, but homestays with the locals can add unforgettable memories to your journey. This includes the typical hill-tribe houses on stilts, where visitors sleep next to the owners on the same floor, eat with them, listen to stories and get recommendations about the place. There are many offers to book online if you search for homestays, with English-speaking owners and reviews by other foreign guests. For a more local experience, look out for 'homestay' signs (written in English) as you travel around. A tent is also a good choice if you like to get up in the middle of nowhere, listening to birdsong or the chatter of farmers working in a nearby field.

The Happy Road

**HOW A LEGENDARY
ROAD CAME TO BE**

In recent years, Ha Giang has become a favourite road trip of adventurous travellers, both for its magnificent rice-terrace fields and the stunning Dong Van Karst Plateau, a Unesco-designated geopark. The construction of 'The Happy Road' is an epic tale of sacrifice and the human spirit.

People Power

Before the road, the Dong Van Karst Plateau was all but unknown. Rocky mountain ranges blocked entry to outsiders and kept tens of thousands of minority people hemmed in. For generations they climbed over mountain paths, on foot and sometimes on horseback. A trip to the nearest town could take a month. Life was remote and difficult, with short supplies of food and clean water.

After relative peace came to the North, in 1959 the government decided to build a road to connect Ha Giang's centre with Dong Van Karst Plateau, including the districts of Quan Ba, Yen Minh, Dong Van and Meo Vac, to help eliminate their poverty.

It was no easy task. In nearly 80 years of dominion, the French had attempted it, but only managed to build 17km. Tens of thousands of volunteers from 16 minority groups in eight northern provinces joined in to help their poor brothers and sisters, armed only with basic tools like hammers, eight-sided crowbars, hoes, shovels and some explosives, carving out the road centimetre by centimetre.

The geography of these mountains, valleys and streams often meant a hundred metres of road took several months to build. But the greatest difficulty came after a thousand days of construction, when the workers faced Ma Pi Leng, the highest peak at 2000m. In the Hmong language, Ma Pi Leng means 'the bridge of a horse's nose', implying the shape of the peak. Continuing the road required carving out a mountain pass with just basic tools – and so the legend of 'The Happy Road' was born.

Left Motorcyclist, Ha Giang **Middle** Quan Ba Mountain **Right** Nho Que River

On the Cliff Face

A 'suicide' squad of 17 was assembled. They climbed the cliffs of Ma Pi Leng, tied themselves by rope to a big old tree to hang on a cliff some 56m from the peak, and started working. Along with the tents went coffins, as many made the ultimate sacrifice.

These brave souls bored small holes into the cliff with crowbars and hammers and placed explosives inside. As each explosion broke a block of rock the size of a football, their happiness also broke out. The squad then received a drill to quicken the pace, finishing their work on the cliff face for the 22km Ma Pi Leng Pass in 11 months.

> Tens of thousands of volunteers from 16 minority groups in eight northern provinces joined in, carving out the road centimetre by centimetre.

Sacrifice for Happiness

During the postwar hardships, for thousands of days, the workers' meals consisted of just rice, vegetables and salt, and they slept in shacks. The lack of water was the greatest difficulty. Additionally, they also faced mosquitoes and malaria, not to mention the threat of death from falling rocks or other accidents. Fourteen members of the squad rest there forever.

After six years of carving out nearly 3 million cu metres of rock, the 200km-long and 4.5m-wide road was completed in 1965, paving a new way and life for the northern people and opening the country's most remote corner to millions of travellers.

◉ Best of Dong Van Karst Plateau

Nho Que River The impossibly green river, which flows at the foot of the challenging Ma Pi Leng Pass, provides an exceptional location for kayaking and stand-up paddleboarding.

Quan Ba Mountain This breast-shaped 'twin mountain' in the heart of a green valley is particularly picturesque and a real feat of nature.

Dong Van's old quarter Home to dozens of adobe houses that are about 100 years old, belonging to the Hmong, Tay, Dao, Nung and other ethnic groups.

12 Be a Farmer
FOR A DAY

FARM LIFE | CULTURE | FOOD

■■■■ Becoming a farmhand for one day – working in a peaceful field or on a farm – makes for a novel and fun escape from the busy modern city. By participating in common farm activities such as ploughing, planting vegetables, cattle breeding and more, you also learn about the life of the north's countryfolk, who initiated the wet-rice civilisation of Vietnam.

BA VI HOMESTEAD ©

🗺 How to

Getting here After arriving in the main town of a province, rent a motorbike or hire a motorbike taxi to reach the villages around which the activities are offered.

When to go Year-round; activities vary depending on the harvest. Better avoid July and August when it's very hot and rainy.

What to wear Wear comfortable clothes and shoes and be ready to get dirty.

NGUYEN LE DIEM/LONELY PLANET ©

Cultivation Wade in knee-deep mud to plough with a buffalo, bail water from a ditch to the field with a bamboo bailer, or try sowing, removing grass and harvesting – it all helps to learn about traditional farming, and to appreciate the local phrase for farmers' work: 'Selling the face to the land and selling the back to the sky'. Moreover, getting grains of white rice ready for cooking also requires turns of milling, pounding and screening, which takes a lot of sweat but can be fun like a special workout.

Fishing How do you fill a cast net with just a bamboo basket or stick, the traditional method of local fishers? Their secret is revealed with some tricks, such as when to calm the water and when to stir it in order to catch the smart fish. Then you're guided to cook your 'best trophy' and enjoy it.

Planting and milking Interested in taking care of plants and animals? Learning to hoe and water vegetables correctly, or to feed and milk a cow or a goat, will provide that joy.

Weaving and embroidering Learn to make the hill tribes' fine, colourful brocade clothing from flax or cotton plants with your own hands.

Growing corn and making corn wine After seeding corn, selecting the best kernels, boiling, fermenting and distilling them into wine with the natural enzyme made from *hong mi* tree seeds, you can relax and enjoy some fragrant, flavourful shots from the mountain and forest.

Top & bottom left Ba Vi homestead

≋ Where to Go

Ba Vi homestead, Hanoi region The work involves a combination of rice and vegetable cultivation, plus making delicious *banh cuon* (steamed rice rolls with minced pork and mushrooms).

Moc Chau dairy farm, Son La province Dairy production and tasting some of the best local products, including yogurt from cow's and goat's milk.

Mai Chau (Hoa Binh province); Ta Phin and Lao Chai villages (Sapa); Nam Dam commune (Ha Giang) On spontaneous request, many villagers are willing to teach you their terrace-field farming techniques, weaving skills and Dao people's well-known herbal baths.

Yen Duc village or Quan Lan Island, Quang Ninh province Try being a fisher and homemade-seafood chef.

13

Drifting on
BA BE LAKE

NATURE | PADDLEBOARDING | CULTURE

▬▬▬ Paddleboarding is a leisurely way to explore Vietnam's largest natural lake in the heart of Ba Be National Park. With limestone mountains soaring above the water, this 'Halong Bay on land' is an ideal camping destination. It's endowed with a diverse ecosystem of rivers, waterfalls, caves, islands and valleys, along with the traditional culture and legends of hill-tribe villages.

🗺 Trip Notes

Getting here Take buses from Hanoi to Bac Kan City (230km) and from Bac Kan City to Ba Be Lake (70km).

When to go Year-round, but summer is the best time for the fresh air on the lake and in the forest.

What to bring An umbrella and bug spray for unexpected rain and insect bites.

⛺ Camping Sites

Pac Ngoi Village Tay people's houses on stilts amid rice and corn fields beside the lake.

Hoi Xuan Mudflat Views over the lake to the more tranquil Bo Lu village with fewer tourists.

Dau Dang Waterfall (pictured) Adventurers' favourite spot – get into the wild and sleep by the water.

■ Recommended by Doan Manh, *director of Mikan Village Ba Vi @doanmanh2787*

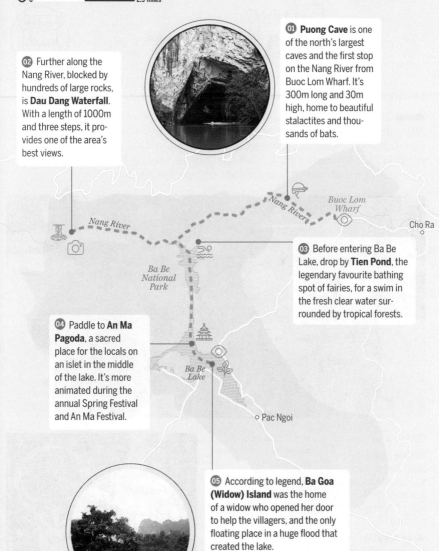

02 Further along the Nang River, blocked by hundreds of large rocks, is **Dau Dang Waterfall**. With a length of 1000m and three steps, it provides one of the area's best views.

01 **Puong Cave** is one of the north's largest caves and the first stop on the Nang River from Buoc Lom Wharf. It's 300m long and 30m high, home to beautiful stalactites and thousands of bats.

Nang River

Buoc Lom Wharf

Nang River

Cho Ra

Ba Be National Park

03 Before entering Ba Be Lake, drop by **Tien Pond**, the legendary favourite bathing spot of fairies, for a swim in the fresh clear water surrounded by tropical forests.

04 Paddle to **An Ma Pagoda**, a sacred place for the locals on an islet in the middle of the lake. It's more animated during the annual Spring Festival and An Ma Festival.

Ba Be Lake

o Pac Ngoi

05 According to legend, **Ba Goa (Widow) Island** was the home of a widow who opened her door to help the villagers, and the only floating place in a huge flood that created the lake.

Ethnic
MARKET

CULTURE | SHOPPING | CUISINE

▬▬▬ At Bac Ha, Vietnam's biggest ethnic market, different minority people gather to offer their domestic and homemade products, trading in everything from brocade to buffalo. Appearing in their traditional hill-tribe clothing, the villagers flock in to enjoy the market like a special weekly festival – a unique showcase of colour and vibrancy in the northern mountains.

CEZARY WOJTKOWSKI/SHUTTERSTOCK ©

🗺 How to

Getting here Bac Ha is about 100km from Sapa and 50km from Lao Cai's centre. Buses to and from both of these places run every day.

When to go Only Sunday mornings; better go early to make the most of it before the market closes around 2pm.

Get the real deal Products made in China are also available, so make sure to get the authentic embroidered ones.

TONY ALBELTON/SHUTTERSTOCK ©

ARGENTOZENO_TH/SHUTTERSTOCK ©

Far left Hmong women, Bac Ha **Below** Hmong necklaces **Near left** Hmong skirts

Horses and buffalo See the two 'best friends' of the mountainous farmers up close. The country's only horse market features the best of various breeds, used either for transport or racing. It's also the region's largest buffalo market, where these animals are sold for farm work, mating, fighting or meat.

Brocade kingdom The market's most colourful corner has handmade products of Hmong women, who are taught how to weave, dye and embroider their own clothes from plants by their mothers and grandmothers at an early age. You can find nice souvenirs and gifts – skirts, head scarves, bags, wall hangings etc, in popular patterns of square, diamond, spiral and more – all expressing imagination and desire for a warm and bright life.

Farming tools All basic and important tools used in the fields, such as various kinds of machetes, ploughshares, hoes or bamboo backpacks (also handmade), demonstrate the typical agricultural production in these mountains, like an open-air museum.

Yummy corner Among dozens of food stalls gathered together, you can't miss the strong-smelling *thang co* (traditional mixed horse meat and organs, the northwest's most typical speciality), but trying it requires courage. Dried sour *pho* mixed with peanuts and herbs is a new experience, totally different from the classic *pho*. *Men men* (traditional corn rice) and *banh duc ngo* (plain corn flan) are other popular dishes.

Real Deals at the Market

Batik Hmong skirts Hmong women's traditional skirts will add a bold, authentic part of Vietnam to your wardrobe.

Spiritual Hmong necklaces Designed like tribal locks (possibly with keys); Hmong people believe they make the soul stay with the body and drive away evil spirits.

Wooden dolls Wearing lively traditional brocade clothes, these handmade miniatures are the creation of skilful local women.

Old buffalo bells Small bronze bells, used to manage buffalo in the fields, make an exceptional souvenir or a creative wind chime.

Tribal
COLOUR

01 Hmong
Colourful shirts and pleated skirts are usually decorated with beads and silver coins. The most popular are red, black and yellow, with square, rhomb or spiral patterns.

02 Muong
A white headscarf and long black skirt with a colourful waistband are essential. A white, blue, pink or brown shirt goes over a colourful top.

03 Thai
A shirt with two central rows of symmetrical butterfly-shaped buttons, a colourful brocade headscarf and a long black skirt with a green waistband.

04 Tay
Similar to *ao dai* (the national dress of Vietnam); everything is black, including the headscarf, highlighted by a shining silver collar.

05 Red Dao
Five colours (red, black, yellow, green and white) on embroidered threads embellish the black

shirt – especially red, the symbol of happiness and luck.

butterfly-shaped button at the neck symbolises happiness.

pants and a colourful headscarf.

Lo Lo kingdom, is indispensable.

06 Nung
A black shirt with coloured sleeves and hem, usually blue and white with triangle and rhomb patterns. A

07 Giay
A shirt in white, pink, red, green or blue, with the neck part in different colours, combined with wide black

08 Lo Lo
Colourful pieces of cloth and embroidery are added to black shirts and pants. A triangle pattern, the symbol of the ancient

09 Ha Nhi
A hat with tassels and a black dress with red, yellow, white and green embroidery on the sleeves.

Mountain & Forest
TASTE

FOOD | CULTURE | ETHNIC GROUPS

▬▬▬ Northern Vietnam's mountains and forests not only provide the lush scenery of the region but also bring special ingredients to the local kitchen. Moreover, the diverse hill tribes, with their long traditions, have maintained and passed on secret recipes of dishes with strong and distinctive flavours that can't be found anywhere else.

QUA TRAM RESTAURANT ©

🍽 How to

When to eat Any time from 7am to 11pm, the opening hours of most restaurants. Check for local markets, which are often only weekly or seasonal.

Best time to go During local festivals, when tradi-tional and typical dishes are available and possibly free for guests.

Be brave Sometimes you need to close your eyes and hold your nose but open your mouth for the best taste. No pain, no gain.

HOANG DINH NAM / STAFF/GETTY IMAGES ©

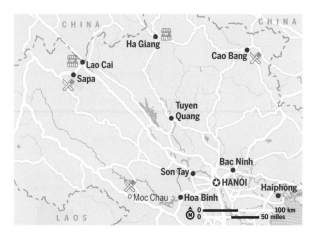

Trau gac bep Pieces of buffalo meat are mixed with strong spices and hung over the fireplace for months to be smoked whenever a meal is prepared. It's shredded into small bits for beer snacks or delicious bites.

Lap xuong Cao Bang Sausage made from black pork mixed with rice wine and spices is dried in the sun and smoked. It's the best-known speciality of Cao Bang's people, with a distinct taste.

Be chao The Moc Chau Plateau is the best place to try this soft, sweet-and-savoury dish of deep-fried veal cooked with oil and bean paste.

Seven-plate salmon Sashimi and six other salmon dishes are offered in the Moc Chau Plateau, including soup, spring roll, grill, crispy fried skin, hotpot and porridge.

Thang co The traditional stew of Hmong people is a mixture of bones and internal organs of the horse. Buffalo, cows and pigs are added later. Hold your nose for a combination of flavours on your tongue: sweet, sour, salty and a bit spicy.

Nam pia The soup speciality at Thai people's festivals is a combination of cow's or goat's intestines. Overcoming the smell and initial bitter taste, you get the sweet and fat flavour as a reward.

Ant-eggs rice cake Tay people's typical food is made from young black ant eggs and fig leaves stuffed inside steamed sticky rice. Very greasy and high in protein.

Top left Cao Bang sausage **Bottom left** *Thang co* preparation, Lao Cai

✔ **Where to Eat**

Peach Garden Salmon Restaurant, Moc Chau Plateau Famous for fresh, delicious salmon and a nice town view.

Ngon Restaurant, Cao Bang Many typical dishes from the region are offered here, especially ant-eggs rice cake.

A Phu Restaurant, Sapa The 100-dish menu includes *thang co* and salmon hotpot – one of Sapa's specialities.

Local markets, Lao Cai and Ha Giang Best places to see *thang co* prepared in big hotpots as well as sample from different BBQ choices.

■ **Recommended by Nguyen Linh,** *former marketing manager of Qua Tram Mountainous Speciality Restaurant*

Listings

BEST OF THE REST

Historic Sights

Hmong King's Palace

Visit the palace of Hmong King Vuong Duc Chinh in Ha Giang province, built in 1898 over 3000 sq metres, to admire its unique architecture with Hmong, Chinese and French influences.

Hoang A Tuong Castle

The mansion of Tay chief Hoang A Tuong in Bac Ha, built in 1914, is a curious combination of styles, from the arch and pillar design and bay-laurel patterns to the Chinese square structure and feng shui on a large hill to the southeast.

Pao's House

Appearing in the well-known local movie *Story of Pao,* this home of four generations that's over 100 years old is typical for the architecture and lifestyle of the Hmong people in Ha Giang province. Features include wooden doors, rock walls and fences, tiled roofs and plum trees in the yard.

Love Markets

Sapa

Held on Saturday evenings for Hmong and Dao people to come and find a partner. While women appear in their best dress, men play music with a leaf or *khen* (pan pipe), to win their heart. Then they may talk, participate in traditional dances and games together, and soon prepare for a wedding.

Khau Vai

Based on a legend of a couple from two different groups who broke up for the peace of their families and society, it has been organised annually on the 26th and 27th days of the third lunar month for a century. Also known as 'affair market', this is a once-a-year chance for former lovers to meet without their partner's jealousy.

Drinks with a View

Haven Sapa Coffee $

From a hill in Cat Cat village, embrace the Sapa scenery of mountain ranges, terrace fields and small roofs under the blue sky.

Viet Trekking Home Sapa $

Enjoy a cup of coffee in the centre of Sapa, admiring the Hoang Lien Son range in the sea of clouds, the Muong Hoa Valley and an occasional mountain train passing by.

Nui Cam $

Observe the town of Ha Giang and the Lo River with a mountainous background at this cafe located halfway to the top of Cam Mountain.

Sky Bar $

The open-air space on the 16th floor of Royal Lotus Hotel offers panoramic views of Halong City and the bay along with a classic cocktail or two.

NGUYEN LE DIEM/LONELY PLANET ©

Kim Boi Hot Spring

Doi Gio Wind Chill $

On a hill surrounded by strawberry fields, this cafe affords the best views of the pine forest and Ang village in the Moc Chau Plateau.

 Green Spaces

Cat Ba National Park

Discover the park's tropical forest and marine ecosystems, and many plants and mammals including the endangered white-headed langur and colourful coral reefs.

Cuc Phuong National Park

Explore ancient caves and Muong villages, or see hundreds of butterflies of various kinds as they wake up from their long winter sleep in April and May.

Ba Vi National Park

Stroll through pine forest, hills of Japanese sunflowers and a glass-dome cactus garden.

Tam Dao National Park

Hike to three peaks, through a misty bamboo forest and to the Hell Pagoda, known for mysterious tales.

Xuan Son National Park

Watch hundreds of kinds of birds gathering or transiting here between October and March as they escape the cold of the north by heading down south.

 Island Beaches

Cat Ba Archipelago

Swim and kayak in Lan Ha Bay, visit Cai Beo (one of Vietnam's largest floating villages), and play with the monkeys on Monkey Island.

Quan Lan Island

Lie on smooth white-sand beaches on the edge of a pine forest and enjoy seafood

Co To Island

specialities like sea urchins, sea cucumbers and thunder crabs.

Co To Island

Crystal-clear turquoise water, along with the peaceful fishing life here, makes for an ideal escape from the busy, dusty city.

 Natural R&R

Kim Boi Hot Spring

Have a nice bath at 34°C to 36°C surrounded by karst mountains and forest in Hoa Binh province. The water is good for both drinking and bathing, and for the treatment of various illnesses, thanks to its high mineral content.

Kenh Ga Hot Spring

Regarded as 'saint water' by the people of Ninh Binh province for its magical effect on injuries and some health problems, thanks to the presence of a lot of minerals.

Quang Hanh Hot Spring

Choose between public (outdoor) and private (indoor) baths, along with massages and physical treatments at this hot spring in Quang Ninh province.

 Scan to find more things to do in Northern Vietnam online

CENTRAL VIETNAM

HISTORIC TOWNS | CAVES | MOTORBIKING

Experience Central Vietnam online

Na Meo

Nam Dinh

Ninh Binh

Paddle through the river canyons of **Tam Coc** or **Trang An** (p120)
🚣 *15min from Ninh Binh*

Thanh Hoa

Dong Tau

Tinh Gia

Nam Can

Hoa Binh

Tan Ky

Dien Chau

Do Luong

Vinh

Cau Treo

Ha Tinh

Ky Anh

Quang Trach

Unearth underground cave kingdoms in **Phong Nha** (p110)
🚐 *45min from Dong Hoi*

Cha Lo

Phong Nha-Ke Bang National Park

THAILAND

LAOS

CENTRAL VIETNAM
Trip Builder

Take a motorbike ride over the **Hai Van Pass** (p122)
🏍 *45min from Danang*

▬▬ Central Vietnam looks a little like a teetering ice-cream cone: narrow at the bottom and bulbous at the top. The slender south is where you'll find the urban delights of Hue, Danang and Hoi An. Moving north, you'll encounter gigantic caves, meandering rivers and cultivated countryside.

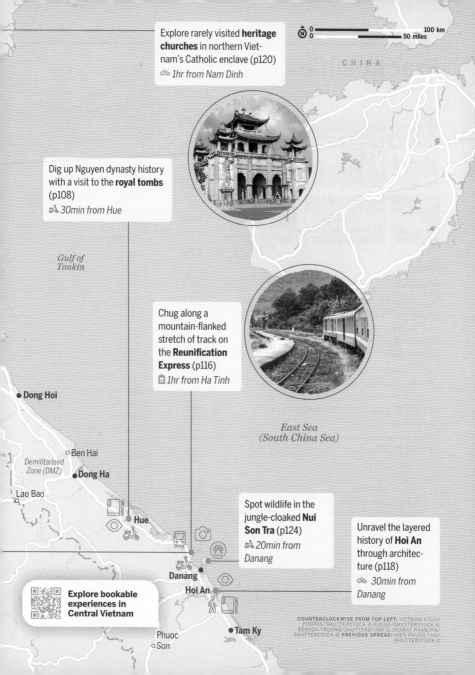

Explore rarely visited **heritage churches** in northern Vietnam's Catholic enclave (p120)

🚗 1hr from Nam Dinh

CHINA

0 — 100 km
0 — 50 miles

Dig up Nguyen dynasty history with a visit to the **royal tombs** (p108)

🏍 30min from Hue

Gulf of Tonkin

Chug along a mountain-flanked stretch of track on the **Reunification Express** (p116)

🚆 1hr from Ha Tinh

East Sea (South China Sea)

● Dong Hoi

○ Ben Hai

Demilitarised Zone (DMZ)

● Dong Ha

Lao Bao

Hue

Spot wildlife in the jungle-cloaked **Nui Son Tra** (p124)

🏍 20min from Danang

Unravel the layered history of **Hoi An** through architecture (p118)

🚗 30min from Danang

Danang

Hoi An

Explore bookable experiences in Central Vietnam

Phuoc ○ Son

● Tam Ky

Practicalities

ARRIVING

Airports Da Nang International Airport serves Danang and Hoi An, Phu Bai Airport serves Hue, and Dong Hoi Airport serves Phong Nha. Taxis to your final destination won't usually cost more than 500,000d.

Train and bus All of Vietnam's major coastal cities are served by train and bus (note: Hoi An doesn't have a train station). Stations are reasonably central; a taxi to your final destination won't cost more than 100,000d.

HOW MUCH FOR A

bowl of noodles
35,000d

coffee
20,000d

motorbike for
the day
150,000d

GETTING AROUND

From city to city Trains will take you to the major cities in central Vietnam, and buses will take you everywhere else.

Within cities and towns Danang, Hue and Hoi An are walkable, though you'll need taxis and motorbike taxis, which are ubiquitous, to get to far-flung corners. Motorbikes and bicycles are also well worth considering. They're cheap and easy to rent through your hotel.

WHEN TO GO

JAN–FEB
Cold, cloudy and a little wet; occasional light storms.

MAR–APR
Sunny, warm, with not too much rain. Good time to visit.

MAY–SEP
Hot, bright and sunny; good if you can handle heat.

OCT–DEC
Very wet with infrequent typhoons. Avoid if you can.

EATING & DRINKING

Regional flavours draw on the wider national profile, though with more chilli. Food tends to be more flavoursome than northern fare and less sweet than most southern dishes. Hue has a deluge of specialities from the region, including *bun bo* (pictured top right), *banh Hue* (pictured bottom right) and *com hen*. Danang and Hoi An also have a strong food history; specialities include *my quang* and *com ga* (see p114). Vietnamese food elsewhere tends to be more basic, though still good. International cuisine is often poor outside Danang and Hoi An, though passable in Hue and Phong Nha. Unless you're dining in Hoi An, booking is rarely needed.

Best cocktails
Craftsman Cocktail Bar, Danang (p128)

Must-try coffee
T Roaster, Hue (p128)

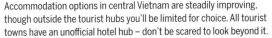

BOOKING TICKETS

Booking most transport tickets can be done entirely online. For the train, visit dsvn.vn. For plane and bus, go to the respective company websites.

WHERE TO STAY

Accommodation options in central Vietnam are steadily improving, though outside the tourist hubs you'll be limited for choice. All tourist towns have an unofficial hotel hub – don't be scared to look beyond it.

Town/City	Where to Stay
Hoi An	Try to stay as close to the old town as possible, or at An Bang beach.
Danang	For modern city vibes, choose a place near or on Đ Bach Dang. If opting for the beach, try to stay close to Đ Vo Nguyen Giap.
Hue	Most accommodation is south of the river, though the north side is prettier and more local.
Phong Nha	Find a place right on the river and take advantage of morning swims and sunset views.
Ninh Binh	There's a good selection of city hotels, and some rather lovely garden options close to Tam Coc.

CONNECT & FIND YOUR WAY

Wi-fi and data Cafes, restaurants and hotels across the region offer free wi-fi. Pick up a SIM with data in any network store; Viettel tends to offer the best coverage in rural areas. The sales assistant can register the SIM for you.

Navigation Addresses can be confusing, but the pin on Google maps, the app most commonly used in Vietnam, is usually right.

MONEY

Most midrange and high-end hotels, restaurants and shops take cards in central Vietnam. Carry cash for everywhere else. ATMs are plentiful in cities and towns but they can be hard to come by in rural areas.

16

Two-Day Tomb
EXPEDITION

MOTORBIKING | HISTORY | COUNTRYSIDE

Hiding in the hills and masked in moss, Hue's royal tombs feel like the stuff of legend. But despite their mythical air, they document an engrossing period of history that covers the beginning and end of the Nguyen dynasty, Vietnam's last monarchical family. Most visitors only visit two or three tombs. This two-day itinerary takes in six in the same order that they were constructed.

🗺 Trip Notes

When to go Hue is not known for its good weather. It can be brutally hot in the summer and relentlessly rainy in the winter. However, unless the city is flooding, this tour is possible all year round.

What to bring Other than the obvious – water, sunscreen, raincoat and good shoes – you might also want to bring a picnic to avoid coming back to town for lunch. You'll spy plenty of pit stops serving coffee, sugar-cane juice and soft drinks.

🚲 Hop on a Bike

If you're an active traveller who's happy to brave the heat (and rain), exploring Hue's tombs by bicycle is a great alternative to motorbike. The roads are good, the traffic is manageable and moving slowly through the countryside gives extended glimpses of local life. You'll still need a reliable mountain bike, so rent a good one or arrange a tour.

■ **Recommended by Shi Jang,** tour guide and co-founder of *Oriental Sky Travel*
@shi_jang

04 Tu Duc was a romantic poet with an affinity for nature, evidenced by the sweeping lake, graceful pavilion and lush trees. **Tu Duc Tomb** makes for a romantic start to the second day.

05 Rarely visited but with excellent views, **Dong Khanh Tomb** has notable European touches, reflecting decades of French colonialism and cultural influence.

03 The elegant little **Thieu Tri Tomb**, which cleanly separates the temple and crypt, provides a pleasant finisher for the first day on your way back into town.

06 Finish the second day with an afternoon visit to the wackiest tomb of the bunch. **Khai Dinh Tomb** hugs a hillside and meshes Vietnamese, Chinese, French and Cambodian styles with debatable degrees of success.

Chau Chu Village

Tuan Village

02 After lunch, head to the dignified and symmetrical **Minh Mang Tomb**, which stretches to a small hill where Minh Mang, one of Vietnam's most powerful emperors, is buried.

01 Start day one with **Gia Long Tomb**, the oldest, furthest and loneliest in the collection. Take the morning to wander around the gigantic crumbling structures and serene lotus ponds.

Hue

Đ Dien Bien Phu

Song Huong (Perfume River)

Song Huu Trach

Song Ta Trach

0 — 2 km
0 — 1 mile
N

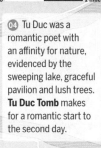

17

Enter the
UNDERWORLD

CAVING | CAMPING | ADVENTURE

Harbouring the biggest caves on the planet, Phong Nha-Ke Bang National Park is a flourishing adventure-tourism hub and one of Vietnam's standout outdoors destinations. The caves, which offer a plethora of experiences, are the star attraction.

Top left Rowboat. Phong Nha-Ke Bang National Park **Top right** Inside Son Doong Cave **Bottom right** Campsite, En Cave (p112)

🗺️ How to

When to go The best time to visit is between March and September. January and February can be a little cold. Most caves are closed October to December.

How to visit Visiting the caves in the national park is strictly con-trolled for safety and conservation reasons and, except for Paradise Cave, you can't explore them independently.

Tour companies Oxalis Adventure (oxalis.com. vn) and Jungle Boss Tours (junglebosstours. com) are the two leading tour operators.

Spoilt for Choice

From ambitious multi-day adventures to leisurely half-day jaunts, there are caving experiences in and around Phong Nha to suit everyone. Here is an expansive (but not exhaustive) list of what's on offer.

Son Doong Cave

One of the world's great natural wonders, Son Doong Cave is 9km long, with chambers taller than the Great Pyramid of Giza and two gaping ceiling collapses. Known as dolines, these concavities have birthed extraordinary underground jungles that double as handy campsites. Other than exploring these two subterranean environs, you'll swim in rivers, stroll between stalagmites (some of which are up to 80m high) and scale a 90m wall. An expedition through Son Doong Cave includes

🌿 Cave Conservation

Phong Nha is an example of tourism done right. Before tours were set up in the national park, illegal logging and hunting were rife as the local people couldn't get by on farming alone. Now most of them have stable work in tourism, eliminating the need to loot the jungle.

■ **Insight from Howard Limbert,** *professional caver at Oxalis Adventure @oxalisadventure*

a visit to neighbouring **En Cave**, the third-largest in the world. There are only a few hundred spots for visitors each year, so you'll need to book many months in advance to avoid disappointment. The tours run for four full days.

Pygmy Cave

If you don't have the time, cash or forethought for Son Doong, Pygmy Cave makes an appealing two-day alternative. Reportedly the planet's fourth-largest cave, Pygmy Cave

is only accessible by an intrepid one-day hike through thick jungle and over karst mountains. You'll arrive and camp in the cave's entrance before exploring its depths the following morning, followed by a two-hour trek through the relentlessly dark and serpentine **Over Cave**. Tip: stay close to your guide to avoid getting lost.

Tu Lan Cave System

More than 20 caves make up the Tu Lan cave system, a handful of which you can explore on

ⓘ The Discovery of Son Doong

Given the cave's magnitude, it's a wonder that Son Doong's discovery was so recent. Local explorer Ho Khanh chanced upon the cave in 1990 when looking for shelter. Once inside the entrance, he heard a thundering river, an indication of the cave's size, but didn't venture any further. After returning home, he didn't think much about the cave until the 2000s, when globetrotting cavers Howard and Deb Limbert were in the area conducting exploratory expeditions. Khanh's story intrigued them and they decided to invite him along. After a few failed attempts, the team rediscovered the cave in 2008 and surveyed it in 2009. They discovered that it contained the biggest chamber of any known cave in the world, making Son Doong, at least by one measure, the biggest cave on the planet.

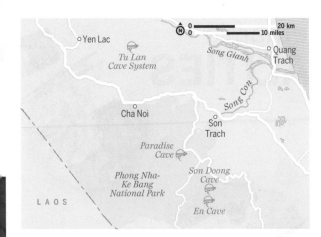

Left Son Doong Cave **Below** Board-walk, Paradise Cave

one-, two-, three- or four-day tours. This is one of the more dynamic caving options, as you'll crawl, climb, swim and ramble in and out of several caves, though none of them are big enough to camp in. This is hardly an issue – the campsites are hemmed in by primary jungle and situated near rivers and rock pools for late-afternoon paddles. Tu Lan was used as one of the locations in Vietnam for the filming of the Hollywood movie *Kong: Skull Island* (2017).

Paradise Cave

Well-lit and family-friendly Paradise Cave is a reliable destination to spend half a day, beginning with a pleasant stroll (or electric buggy ride) through lush jungle before ascending some steps and entering the underground dominion. The cave stands out for its intricate and elaborate stalagmites, which – due to a raised boardwalk to protect the cave floor – are presented like exhibits in a museum. Although the cave system extends for 31km, most people only visit the first kilometre. If you don't feel like camping in the jungle or you're travelling with little ones, Paradise Cave fits the bill better than most.

Central Vietnam's
SPECIALITIES

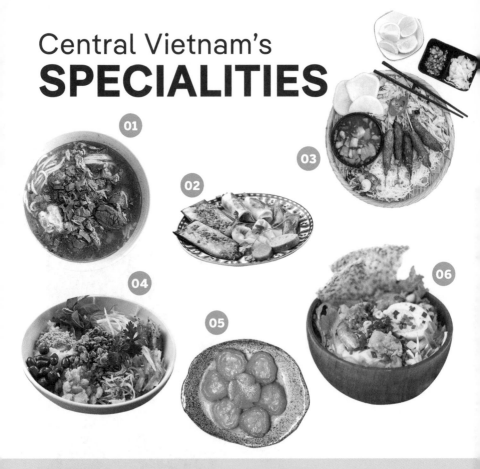

01 *Bun bo Hue*

A spicy beef noodle soup seasoned with lemongrass. Hue's favourite breakfast dish.

02 *Banh Hue*

There are several *banh Hue* varieties, which are delicate savoury rice cakes originally concocted for the kings of old.

03 *Nem lui*

Chargrilled pork patties wrapped with salad and pickles. Served with a peanut sauce. Try it in Hue and Danang.

04 *Com hen*

Minuscule muscles served with soupy rice, crackling, peanuts and salad bits. Try it in Hue.

05 *Mon an chay*

Hue is Vietnam's Buddhist capital and hence also its vegan capital, full of great animal-friendly establishments.

06 *My quang*

Central Vietnam's favourite noodle dish is a flat yellow noodle served with meat, seafood and a rice cracker. Try it in Hoi An and Danang.

07 *Cao lau*

Hoi An's speciality noodle dish is thick yellow noodles served with wontons, pork and shrimp.

08 *Com ga Hoi An*

Try Vietnam's best chicken and rice in the centre, especially in Hoi An and Danang. Usually served with a herby onion salad.

09 *Chao canh*

Try this round-noodle soup served with fish, pork and a side of dippable spring rolls in Phong Nha and Dong Hoi.

10 *Chao luon*

Eel soup with bread, popular in the northern-most central provinces. Try it in Nghe An, Ha Tinh or Thanh Hoa.

11 *Hai san*

Hai san means 'seafood', and it's fresh and plentiful anywhere with a beach. Try it anywhere you can see the sea.

12 *Pho Nam Dinh*

Nam Dinh has its own take on Vietnam's national dish. Some argue this is where it originated.

18 All ABOARD!

SLOW TRAVEL | MOUNTAINS | COASTLINE

The Reunification Express is essentially one long track that runs from the Chinese border to Ho Chi Minh City (with a few offshoots). Narrow and hilly, central Vietnam has some especially alluring trackways, from coast-hugging curves to river-hopping bridges. Travelling by train in Vietnam is rarely quicker than bus or car, but taking it slow while absorbing the scenery is part of the experience.

NGUYEN QUANG NGOC TONKIN/SHUTTERSTOCK ©

🗺 How to

Buying tickets Try dsvn. vn for online booking, including seat selection. You can also buy tickets at the train station.

When to go Take advantage of the light and travel during the day for the best bits.

Train classes Most trains have four class types: hard seat, soft seat, six-person sleeper and four-person sleeper.

Where to sit Choose wisely when deciding which side of the carriage to sit in, to make the most of the views.

WAN KUM SEONG/SHUTTERSTOCK ©

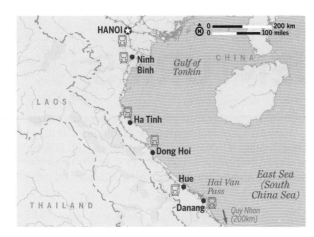

Below are some of the most notable journeys – they assume travelling north to south, but they'd be just as enjoyable in the other direction.

Hanoi to Ninh Binh Escaping Hanoi by train is a unique way to observe the chaotic capital as it swirls over, under and next to the tracks. A bizarre combo of communist and colonial architecture, the **Hanoi Train Station** (p63) is also an iconic place to start. After Hanoi the scenery is rather humdrum until the looming karst mountains of Ha Nam and Ninh Binh start to emerge. (Sit on the west side of the carriage.)

Ha Tinh to Dong Hoi The northern part of the region (Thanh Hoa, Nghe An and Ha Tinh) is devoid of any popular highlights, so most travellers opt instead to take a flight or overnight train between the north and the centre. In both cases, they miss this spectacular, mountain-flanked stretch of track, which moves away from the coast in Ha Tinh before entering Quang Binh and descending to Dong Hoi. These hills are home to several Christian communities, evidenced by the picturesque, pointed church steeples. (Sit on the east side of the carriage.)

Hue to Danang Combining craggy coastline with forested mountains, the track between Hue and Danang offers spellbinding vistas of lagoons, beaches, islets and villages. The highlight is the **Hai Van Pass**, where the track clings to mountains that caress the sea. If you're lucky, the train will stop briefly for a view of **Lang Co Beach**, a pretty stretch of white sand on the north side of the pass. (Sit on the east side of the carriage.)

Top left Hai Van Pass **Bottom left** Hanoi Train Station

Vintage Travel on *The Vietage*

For a lavish experience, *The Vietage* (thevietage train.com) connects Danang with Quy Nhon on the south-central coast with unabashed nostalgia for the era of romantic rail travel. The opulent 12-person carriage offers gourmet dining, a cocktail bar, head and shoulder massages, free-flow drinks and private, two-person compartments. *The Vietage* leaves Danang for Quy Nhon each morning and makes the return journey in the evening. The trip in one direction takes a little over six hours.

19

One Town, Five
CENTURIES

ARCHITECTURE | HISTORY | NATURE

A stroll around Hoi An, by far Vietnam's best-preserved old town, is a rare opportunity to walk back through the centuries. But wandering through the pretty, lantern-lit streets won't just help you unwrap the area's various historical eras; it will also unpack the foreign architectural and artistic influences on the town.

🏛 My Son Sanctuary

Step further back in time at My Son (pictured), ancient religious ruins about 40km west of Hoi An. Built by the Cham people, some of the buildings are almost 2000 years old. A visit here is as much about the setting as it is about history: behind the moss-covered temples, separated by lavish jungle and trickling streams, the forested hills of the central highlands loom.

🗺 Trip Notes

Tickets The Hoi An old town is ticketed, with booths set up at every entry point. You may also need to show tickets at some of the attractions.

Getting around Walking is the only option, since cars and motorbikes are banned (thankfully). You'll come across plenty of cafes, restaurants and shops as you move around.

Guide or no guide A guide is unnecessary except when visiting My Son, where printed information is both poor and scarce.

05 The projects of Vo Trong Nghia, the darling of Vietnam's biophilic architecture movement, employ natural materials and embed plants into the structure. An example is Hoi An's **Atlas Hotel**.

01 First built in the 1590s by merchants from Japan, Hoi An's iconic **Japanese Covered Bridge** is one of the town's oldest structures (though it was rebuilt and adapted over the centuries).

02 A 17th-century Chinese assembly hall opposite 35 Tran Phu was later converted into a **temple** honouring sea goddess Thien Hau. Bursting with colour, it has pink bricks, green tiles and a golden altar.

My Son (37km)

Đ Tran Hung Dao

Đ Hung Vuong

Đ Nguyen Thi Minh Khai

Đ Duong Cao Hong Lanh

Đ Cong Nu Ngoc Hoa

Đ Dao Duy Tu

Đ Le Loi

Đ Nguyen Hue

O L D   T O W N

Đ Nguyen Duy Hieu

Đ Truong Minh Luong

Đ Tran Phu

Đ Nguyen Thai Hoc

Đ Bach Dang

Cam Nam Bridge

An Hoi Peninsula

04 Built in the 18th century, **Tan Ky House** has notable Chinese and Japanese influences. The exquisite detailing includes Chinese poems written in inlaid mother-of-pearl.

03 In the 19th and 20th centuries, the French colonisers made a lasting impact on Hoi An's architecture. **Tran Duong House** is an eye-catching example of ornate terraced housing with balconies.

Thu Bon River

N

0   500 m
0   0.25 miles

20 Christian VIETNAM

CHURCHES | VILLAGES | COUNTRYSIDE

CENTRAL VIETNAM EXPERIENCES

Church-hopping probably isn't the first experience that comes to mind on a trip to Vietnam – but that's one of the best reasons for this itinerary. The northern part of central Vietnam remains a stronghold of Christianity, evidenced by the magnificent old churches that speckle Nam Dinh province. And yet you're unlikely to see any other visitors, international or domestic.

SUZANA TRAN/SHUTTERSTOCK ©

🗺 Trip Notes

Where from Base yourself in one of the nearby cities of Nam Dinh or Ninh Binh and explore from there.

How long You'll need a full day to cover all five churches (as well as any others that appeal en route).

Mode of transport Car or motorbike. If you're considering a guide, this is best arranged in Hanoi. Companies will also arrange a car and driver.

⛵ River Cruises

The day after (or before) exploring the churches, it's worth tagging on a two-hour cruise along the river systems of Ninh Binh, the area's prime attraction. There are two to choose from: **Trang An** (pictured) and **Tam Coc**. Both cruises meander through karst mountains and caves.

0 / 20 km
0 / 10 miles

Nam Dinh

Ninh Binh

Ho Hoan Kiem

Xuan Thuy

Yen Dinh

01 A pretty and symmetrical church built in the 1920s, **Trung Linh** is a popular spot for wedding photography shoots.

02 You can spend the better part of an hour exploring the gigantic, castle-like **Hung Nghia**. Get to the top of one of the twin steeples and onto the roof for views of nearby rice paddies.

03 The cinematic church ruins of **Hai Ly** jut dramatically out to sea. Both the structure and the land beneath are severely eroded, but many ornate details remain.

Phat Diem

Thinh Long

05 The magnificent **Phat Diem** blends European and Asian architecture. From this stone church, Fowler observes his first battle in Graham Greene's *The Quiet American*.

04 A short stroll inland and away from Hai Ly, the yellow church of **Xuong Dien** has borrowed elements from Vietnamese Buddhist temples to craft an unusual and attractive facade.

TOP: MINHHUE/SHUTTERSTOCK ©
BOTTOM: QUANG VU/SHUTTERSTOCK ©

122

By Tom Divers
Tom is the Ho Chi Minh City–based author of Vietnam Coracle, an independent online travel and motor-biking guide @vietnamcoracle

Motorbiking Vietnam

CREATE YOUR OWN ADVENTURE

Few travel experiences offer the independence of a motorbike road trip. Free from the constraints of public transport and tours, you're the architect of your own itinerary. With planning, awareness of risks and attention to safety, motorbiking Vietnam can be your most memorable journey.

Left Ha Giang Loop **Middle** Protective gear **Right** Riding pillion

A Brief History

Since the 1990s, the motorbike has been the nation's primary mode of transport. As international visitors increased towards the 2000s, independent road trips gained popularity. In 2008, the profile of motorbiking Vietnam was boosted when BBC's *Top Gear* filmed a road-trip episode. Today, what was once the preserve of an intrepid few has become a travel highlight.

A self-drive road trip is an 'open world' adventure, allowing travellers the freedom to choose their own path, stop when and where they like, and explore any region. Riders enjoy unparalleled access to Vietnam's landscapes and cities.

The 'Golden Loop'

Traversing the rugged geological divide between Vietnam's central cities, two roads run parallel at the nation's narrow 'waist'. Scenic and historical, they can be combined to form a round trip known as the 'Golden Loop'.

Straddling the coast, the **Hai Van Pass** curls around a mountainous spur that has served as a boundary of king-doms, cultures and climate for centuries. Paul Theroux enthused about its grandeur after travelling here in 1973. Thirty-five years later, Jeremy Clarkson swept up the hair-pin bends on an old Vespa and many thousands followed in his tyre tracks. Today, the pass is the most popular ride in the country.

Inland, a thread of asphalt winds into the distance with such organic grace that it appears part of the natural landscape. **'Ho Chi Minh Road'** is a name redolent of

XUANHUONGHO/SHUTTERSTOCK ©

SERJ BRK/SHUTTERSTOCK ©

war, but for those who ride it, their lasting impression is of the majesty of nature. Jungles coat mountains like melted wax, rivers fill valleys like veins of cobalt, and limestone pillars rise like crenellated fortifications.

Bookending these roads, Danang, Hoi An and Hue are hubs for motorbike rental, offering convenient one-way pickup and drop-off. While the 'Golden Loop' is an ideal entry point for riders, outstanding routes such as **Ha Giang**, **Phong Nha** and the **Truong Son Dong Road** beckon further afield.

> A thread of asphalt winds into the distance with such organic grace that it appears part of the natural landscape.

Safety

Riding legally, responsibly and with insurance are minimum requirements. Common sense, respect for the risks, extra safety gear, acceptance of personal responsibility and a grasp of local driving culture are essential. In Vietnam, there's a discrepancy between official road rules and the reality of driving practices. Before setting out, riders need an awareness of the rhythm, flow, speed, general conduct and hierarchies of priority on the nation's roads.

Motorbike rental is sophisticated, efficient and reliable. Good companies maintain their motorbikes and provide quality safety equipment, mechanical support and assistance obtaining licences.

Regardless of location, motorbiking has certain innate dangers. Travellers should only undertake a self-drive road trip if they're prepared to accept the risks and responsibility.

✅ Checklist

Legal requirements Local driving licence, helmet, insurance.

Insurance Research your policy in advance – some won't cover motorbiking.

Local driving culture Ride pillion before going solo to get familiar with road etiquette.

Riding Practise first; previous experience is preferable.

Rent, don't buy Good companies maintain their motorbikes to a high standard; the same can't be said when buying.

Rental Tigit Motorbikes (tigitmotorbikes.com), Flamingo Travel (flamingotravel. com.vn), Style Motorbikes (stylemotorbikes.com).

Routes, maps and resources Vietnam Coracle (vietnam coracle.com), rental companies, Google Maps.

Repairs Rental companies offer 24-hour assistance; *sua xe* means 'mechanic'.

Extras Knee/elbow pads, gloves, shoes, day/night glasses, rain suit.

21 O Wild
NIGHT

WILDLIFE | CAMPING | SCENERY

At the top of Nui Son Tra, watch the sun go down on the peninsula as the salty wind howls around you, fall asleep to the birds serenading the stars, and wake up to the brilliant sun rising from the tranquil ocean. The altitude provides cooler temperatures, and the rugged land is rich with flora and fauna. If you're lucky, you might even catch a glimpse of the elusive red-shanked douc.

BEE-EATER/SHUTTERSTOCK ©

🗺 **How to**

Getting here The scenic drive takes approximately 20 minutes from the base of Nui Son Tra on a winding, paved road. You need a semi-automatic or manual motorbike to get to the campsite. For your safety, automatic scooters are prohibited in certain areas of Nui Son Tra.

When to go The best camping weather is December through July.

How much Overnighting at Ban Co Peak is free, but you will need to factor in rental gear, such as a motorbike, tent, sleeping bag and sleeping pad.

MUFTI ADI UTOMO/SHUTTERSTOCK ©

At the northeast corner of Danang lies **Nui Son Tra**, a protected, 44-sq-km reserve with almost 300 types of plants and more than 100 animal species. A winding, steep road cuts through the verdant peninsula with plenty of attractions and picturesque landscapes along the way. One of those attractions is Son Tra's highest point. **Ban Co Peak** stands 693m above sea level and offers breathtaking views of the sprawling city as well as the glistening East Sea (South China Sea). Follow a dirt lane to get to an old helicopter landing pad, now often used as a campsite. As you admire the sunset, city lights and sunrise, keep an eye and an ear out for the wild creatures of the peninsula.

Red-shanked douc The best way to spot the endangered red-shanked douc is to watch for movement in the trees. The aerial specialists love to swing under branches and can easily land jumps up to 6m.

Brown hawk-owl You'll probably hear the brown hawk-owl before you see it, with its soft, musical 'oo-uk...ooo-uk' call at dusk and dawn. To spot one, check the tops of trees and look for small birds that tend to swarm where it roosts.

Reticulated python Up to 9m long, the reticulated python is one of the largest snakes native to Asia. If you see one, just leave it be. They won't attack unless provoked.

Far left Red-shanked douc **Bottom left** Reticulated python **Near left** East Sea (South China Sea) from Ban Co Peak

 Learn More

If you want to venture deep into the plants and wildlife of Nui Son Tra, make your way to **Nature Dance** in Danang. The education centre was created by **GreenViet** (greenviet.org), a non-profit organisation that works to conserve important ecosystems and endangered species of the central Vietnam region. Admission is free.

GreenViet also organises in-depth wildlife tours to Nui Son Tra, as well as volunteering events such as planting trees and clean-up days, which are open to the public.

22 CHASING
Waterfalls

SCENERY | ADVENTURE | COUNTRYSIDE

Get swept away from the chaos of Danang city and venture deep into the quiet countryside. Drive on unkempt dirt roads, traverse the thick jungle and cross bubbling, shallow rivers. At the end of your journey, you'll uncover one of the area's hidden cascades, frolic in the refreshing water, and bask in the beauty of the untouched wilderness.

How to

Getting here All trips require driving and hiking. Depending on the waterfall of choice, drives can take anywhere from one hour to 1½ hours one-way, with trekking times ranging from 15 minutes to 3½ hours one-way.

When to go The best waterfall weather is between January and September.

How much Tours cost between 500,000d and 2,100,000d, but you will need to factor in motorbike rental or driver as well.

The great waterfalls of Danang lie within the mysterious mountains to the west of the city, where the water flows down from natural springs, feeding the rivers that slice through the area and eventually dumping into the East Sea (South China Sea). Tony and Cameron at

Danang Hoi An Waterfalls (danangwaterfalls.com) have spent four years exploring this wild frontier, following waterways and forging paths, and they've chosen to share their favourite cascades with anyone with a sense of adventure, a dash of curiosity and a love for waterfalls.

Top right Dominion Falls, Danang
Bottom right Elephant Springs

≋ DIY Trips

If you want to take yourself on a less gruelling adventure, hit up one of the following water recreation areas: **Suoi Voi (Elephant Springs)**, **Ngam Doi Ecotourism Area** or **Nui Than Tai Hot Springs Park**. All three are easy day trips from Danang.

Tours range from the mild yet picturesque **Fairy Falls** with its easy access, natural pools and shallow cliff jumping, to an overnighter at **Shattered Falls** – likely the biggest waterfall in the Danang area – complete with breathtaking scenery, swimming, cliff diving and rock climbing. But if you want the most bang for your buck, opt for the Dominion tour. It's a series of three waterfalls, including one that flows into a 6m-deep pool.

Bear in mind, these journeys are not for the faint of heart. The thick jungle is unpredictable, the paths are steep and the current can be overwhelming. As such, most of the tours are recommended to physically fit, experienced trekkers. If you're game, you'll get to unlock the secret waterfalls held within the jungles just beyond Danang's city limits.

Listings

BEST OF THE REST

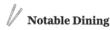 **Notable Dining**

Pub With Cold Beer $

The Pub With Cold Beer serves, you guessed it, cold beer. But people really come for the grilled chicken, which is served with a delicious home-made peanut sauce. It's located in Phong Nha.

Lien Hoa $

Excellent value and immensely popular with Hue locals, Lien Hoa has a gigantic menu of vegan delights. Try the fake chicken drum-sticks or the '12 predestined affinity' salad.

Le Comptoir $$$

A French chef and Italian sommelier join forces to bring an inspired, elegant dining experience to Danang. Arguably the best splurge option in this beachside city.

Nu Eatery $$

A cute little restaurant in Hoi An serving freshly prepared Vietnamese dishes with a modern twist, Nu Eatery has made a name for itself with young and trendy Vietnamese travellers.

 Coffees & Cocktails

T Roaster $

This unassuming cafe is tucked down a quiet street close to Thien Mu Pagoda in Hue; there's also a branch in the centre. It serves the best coffee in the city.

Craftsman Cocktail Bar $$

Danang's first artisanal-cocktail bar was set up by breakdance- and hip-hop-loving local Ho Anh Tuan, who is often found shaking things up behind the bar. The bar, a block back from the beach, specialises in giving Western cocktail classics a Vietnamese twist.

43 Factory $

Around the corner from the Craftsman is 43 Factory, which serves up an assortment of local coffees made with beans from across Vietnam. The menu also includes rich Western coffee with plenty of non-dairy extras.

 Sand & Sea

An Bang

A mix of locals, expats and tourists flock to Hoi An's funkiest beach. The beach further south, nicknamed An Bang Two, is a little quieter.

My Khe

Danang's My Khe is Vietnam's biggest and best metropolitan beach, with deckchairs and sunbeds for rent, coconuts, sugar-cane juice and rows of restaurants serving fresh seafood.

Lang Co

Halfway between Danang and Hue, Lang Co regularly features on lists of the world's most beautiful beaches. Despite all the attention, the major hotel chains are yet to descend on the strip.

An Bang

Vinh Hien

Vinh Hien is a little beach for intrepid adventurers about an hour south of Hue – getting there is half the fun. The beachside restaurants are only frequented by locals, which gives you an opportunity to practise your Vietnamese.

Nhat Le

A lesser-known beach in Dong Hoi, Nhat Le is just an hour from Phong Nha, making it the perfect place to refresh after a crawl through some caves.

Thien Mu Pagoda

 Green Sanctuaries

Ba Na Hills Resort

A counterfeit and kitsch European village in the hills near Danang, Ba Na won't be to everyone's taste. But the cable car journey to get there is enjoyable – and it's home to the Golden Bridge, which is, for better or worse, fast becoming one of Vietnam's most recognisable sights.

Bach Ma National Park

The antithesis to Ba Na Hill Resort, Bach Ma is wild, natural and has a handsome collection of genuine French villas, some of which serve as accommodation. Catch the sunrise before trekking to the thundering Do Quyen Waterfall.

Phong Nha-Ke Bang National Park

Though famous for its caves (p110), Phong Nha-Ke Bang National Park also offers kayaking, cycling, motorbiking and river cruise opportunities.

Pu Mat National Park

A gigantic and lonely area of protected green space that juts into Laos, Pu Mat National Park has picturesque villages, pretty waterfalls and virtually no tourists. Guides are recommended, especially as some parts require permits.

 Religious Sights

Thien Mu Pagoda

Hue's Thien Mu is a picturesque, multilevel pagoda that rises from a sweeping river bend. Time your visit with the sunset if you can.

Tu Hieu Pagoda

One of Hue's oldest and most atmospheric pagodas, Tu Hieu is associated with Thich Nhat Hanh, a Zen master and author of an anthology about modern Buddhism, who passed away in January 2022.

Marble Mountains

In between Danang and Hoi An sit the Marble Mountains (Ngu Hanh Son), a bizarre collection of temples that fill the space left by decades of mining. The manifestation of Buddhist hell, though terrifying, is particularly ornate.

Lady Buddha

Look out to sea from the beach in Danang and you'll spot Lady Buddha to the left at the foot of Nui Son Tra. She's also worth seeing up close, not least of all because the road to get there is so scenic.

 Scan to find more things to do in Central Vietnam online

CENTRAL VIETNAM REVIEWS

SOUTHEAST COAST

BEACHES | DIVING | SEAFOOD

Experience the Southeast Coast online

Pleiku

SOUTHEAST COAST
Trip Builder

With 3260km of coastline, Vietnam has its fair share of beaches, most of them situated on the southeastern coast. Break up your trip with some sea and sun, feasting on fresh seafood, spotting turtles, or simply lazing on palm-fringed beaches.

Enjoy a seafood feast cooked to order on a floating restaurant in **Bong Benh** (p145)
🚗 *35min from Quy Nhon*

Soak in a mineral mud bath at the **Thap Ba Hot Springs** (p152)
🚗 *15min from central Nha Trang*

CAMBODIA

Phan Thiet

Mμ
N

Ho Chi Minh City

Ham Thuan Nam

Phuoc Le

Vung Tau

Climb up a giant **Christ the King statue** for sweeping sea views (p146)
🚗 *25min from central Vung Tau*

Soc Trang

Snorkel in the crystalline waters of **Con Dao** (p149)
✈ *45min from Ho Chi Minh City*

Explore bookable experiences on the Southeast Coast

Con Dao Islands

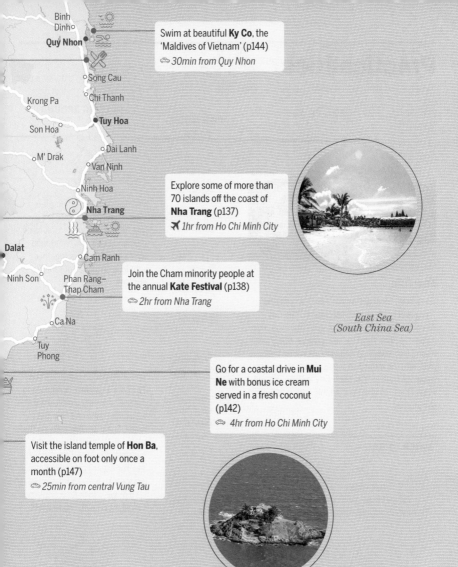

Binh
Dinh
Quy Nhon

Song Cau

Krong Pa
Chi Thanh

Tuy Hoa

Son Hoa

M' Drak
Dai Lanh

Van Ninh

Ninh Hoa

Nha Trang

Dalat

Cam Ranh

Ninh Son
Phan Rang–
Thap Cham

Ca Na

Tuy
Phong

Swim at beautiful **Ky Co**, the 'Maldives of Vietnam' (p144)
🚗 *30min from Quy Nhon*

Explore some of more than 70 islands off the coast of **Nha Trang** (p137)
✈ *1hr from Ho Chi Minh City*

Join the Cham minority people at the annual **Kate Festival** (p138)
🚗 *2hr from Nha Trang*

*East Sea
(South China Sea)*

Go for a coastal drive in **Mui Ne** with bonus ice cream served in a fresh coconut (p142)
🚗 *4hr from Ho Chi Minh City*

Visit the island temple of **Hon Ba**, accessible on foot only once a month (p147)
🚗 *25min from central Vung Tau*

Witness turtle conservation efforts on the uninhabited island of **Bay Canh** (p149)
⛴ *30min from Con Dao*

0   100 km
0   50 miles

Practicalities

ANDREY BURMAKIN/SHUTTERSTOCK ©

ARRIVING

Cam Ranh International Airport serves Nha Trang and is 35km south of the city. Phu Cat Airport is 31km northwest of Quy Nhon. Con Dao Airport is 14km from the town centre. Vung Tau, Phan Thiet and Phan Rang are served by buses and, with the latter two, trains. There are regular minivans from Ho Chi Minh City to Vung Tau and Phan Thiet – a fast, comfortable option to make the journey.

WHEN TO GO

DEC–FEB
Perfect time: pleasant temperatures and sunny skies.

MAR–MAY
The hottest months with little rain. Surf season in Mui Ne.

JUN–AUG
Start of rainy season; high humidity. Turtle season in Con Dao.

SEP–NOV
The wettest months with frequent storms.

HOW MUCH FOR A

private mud bath
425,000d

seafood meal
250,000d

4WD ride on Mui Ne sand dunes
200,000d

GETTING AROUND

Walking Nha Trang, Vung Tau, Phan Thiet and Con Dao are excellent for walking, with restaurants, bars and cafes centred around the main beach area together with long stretches of sand for strolling.

Two wheels Con Dao and Phan Thiet are especially conducive to cycling or driving a motorbike, with little traffic and nice, flat roads. There are even groups that cycle the 100km (10 hours) between Ho Chi Minh City and Vung Tau. For a quick ride, negotiate a price with a *xe om* (motorbike taxi) driver – look for a single person on a bike with two helmets.

Ride-sharing Grab ride-sharing (cars and motorbikes) operates in most of these locations.

EATING & DRINKING

Vietnam's southeastern coast is made for seafood lovers, with sea-to-table fare served everywhere. Restaurants abound where you can pick your live proteins from tanks and have them cooked to order. Steamed in beer? Stir-fried with tamarind? Grilled with scallions? Nothing is off the menu. Nha Trang also has a grilled pork kebab called *nem nuong Nha Trang* (pictured top right), ready to wrap in rice paper with noodles and fresh herbs, while Vung Tau's speciality is *banh khot* (crispy dough topped with squid or shrimp; pictured bottom right).

Best beach food court	Must-try seafood
Pit Stop, Mui Ne (p142)	Hai San Ben Cang, Nha Trang (p153)

TOP: TRIEU NHAT LE/SHUTTERSTOCK ©
BOTTOM: SILUOK/SHUTTERSTOCK ©

CONNECT & FIND YOUR WAY

Wi-fi Most of these destinations are popular with foreign tourists, meaning wi-fi won't be a problem at hotels, guesthouses, restaurants and cafes. Con Dao sometimes experiences spotty connections, but things are improving.

Navigation Shuttles are your friend as they can often drop you off right at your hotel – even airport shuttles if you're centrally located.

MONEY

ATMs abound in these tourist hotspots, so access to cash won't be an issue. Keep in mind that Western food and seafood will strain the budget, as will restaurants catering to tourists.

WHERE TO STAY

From beach shabby to private pool villas, you'll find lodgings for all budgets in any of these coastal towns that are apt for singles, couples and families.

Town	Pro/Con
Quy Nhon	Mini-hotels abound along the 4km stretch of city beach. Look slightly south for luxe options.
Nha Trang	All the action is along Đ Tran Phu. Save money by looking one or two streets back from the beach.
Phan Rang	Consider nearby Ninh Chu Beach for quieter accommodation, especially if you like kite-surfing.
Vung Tau	Front Beach has the best concentration of restaurant and bars. Head east to Long Hai and Ho Tram for seclusion.
Phan Thiet	The Mui Ne tourist strip is where all the restaurants and bars are located.
Con Dao	The centre of town by An Hai Beach has a good mix of mini-hotels and homestays.

PACE YOURSELF

Scheduling a beach getaway is a great way to break up your trip, so give yourself enough time to simply relax and soak up the laid-back vibe.

23 Beaches, Boats & **BATHS**

ISLAND-HOPPING | MUD BATHS | BEACHES

███████ Nha Trang is Vietnam's most popular beach destination, with hundreds of kilometres of coastline, accommodation and attractions lining the 6km-long city beach, and dozens of islands to explore. Direct flights make it popular with Chinese, Russian and Korean tourists, giving the city a multicultural vibe. The location also makes it a nice place to break up a longer tour of Vietnam.

ANDREAS ROSE/SHUTTERSTOCK ©

🗺 **How to**

Getting here Cam Ranh International Airport is 35km south of the city; plenty of taxis and shuttle buses ply the coastal road to town. Trains and overnight buses are also good options.

When to go Nha Trang enjoys warm weather year-round, with the driest, sunniest days from February to May. From September to December, tropical storms may put a damper on beach days.

Avoid the crowds Nha Trang is busy on weekends and over the holidays. Come midweek or in April and May for good weather with fewer people.

VALSIB/SHUTTERSTOCK ©

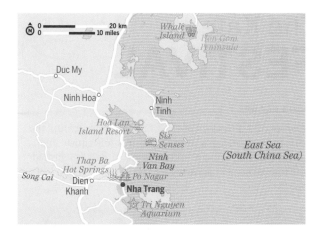

Top left Whale Island **Bottom left** Mineral bath, I-Resort

🦪 **Snorkelling Spots**

The 160-sq-km Hon Mun Marine Protected Area covers nine islands. Home to about 350 species of hard coral and over 230 species of reef fish, it's Nha Trang's best snorkelling and diving area.

Rainbow Reef Many beautifully coloured hard and soft corals from 4m to 12m.

Mama Hanh Beach Sandy shoreline with soft corals and rocky outcrops from 1m to 8m. Great place to see cuttlefish.

Madonna Rock Mainly hard corals from 3m to 12m, with an exciting swim-through at 8m for the adventurous and freedivers.

Cemetery Bay Shallow sandy bottom and one of the few places in Vietnam to see garden eels.

Whale Island Awesome beach and boat snorkelling; a couple of small wooden boats at 8m attract interesting marine life.

■ **Recommended by Jeremy P Stein**, *PADI course director and founder of Rainbow Divers-Vietnam* @jezza.vn

Island-hopping In addition to Nha Trang's family-friendly city beach, there are more than 70 islands to visit. While you can arrange your own boat hire at the **Cau Da Pier**, most visitors go with day trips visiting three or four islands, including lunch and snorkelling, and a stop at the slightly worn **Tri Nguyen Aquarium**. Just be aware that the super-cheap prices are made up by volume, so expect to share a packed boat.

Get muddy Nha Trang has emerged as the unofficial mud-bath capital of Vietnam, with at least four different spots where you can soak in a tub of warm, mineral-enriched mud either privately or grouped with complete strangers. The largest three have similar facilities (mud baths, swimming pools, herbal baths etc). The **100 Egg Theme Park** is the newest, **I-Resort** gets style points, while a visit to the original **Thap Ba Hot Springs** (p152) can be paired with a stop at the nearby ancient **Po Nagar** Cham towers.

Northern escape Travel north of Nha Trang to get away from the crowds and into quiet solitude. The area around Ninh Van Bay is actually a peninsula but feels like a secluded island. Take a speedboat and stay at one of the posh resorts like the ultra-luxe **Six Senses**, or book a boat tour to **Hoa Lan Island Resort** for the day and explore the orchid gardens and laze by the pretty beach. If you have more than a couple of days in Nha Trang, consider spending a few Robinson Crusoe–esque nights on remote **Whale Island**.

24 The Kate
FESTIVAL

CULTURE | FESTIVALS | ETHNIC GROUPS

Honouring deities, heroes and ancestors of the Cham minority group, the annual three-day Kate Festival (pronounced 'kah-tay') features folk music and dancing, wonderfully colourful clothing and age-old religious rituals celebrated in and around three ancient towers near Phan Rang.

JAMES PHAM/LONELY PLANET ©

🗺 How to

When to go The festival takes place on the first day of the seventh month of the Cham calendar, which is typically around September/October. See Visit Vietnam (vietnam. travel) for exact dates.

Where to stay For a truly insider experience, stay at the rustic Inra Champa Homestay, owned by Inra Jaka, one of the leading members of the Cham community in Phan Rang.

Making friends Having snacks to share is a great icebreaker. Bring something to sit on, as there is little to no seating at any of the events.

HECKE61/SHUTTERSTOCK ©

Top left Dance performance, Kate Festival **Bottom left** Po Sah Inu towers

Day 1: Reception of the king's garments The most important festival on the Cham calendar, Mbeng Kate draws the Cham and Raglai people back to their hometowns to join in the festivities. Decked out in their finest garb, often handwoven by village artisans on traditional wooden looms and incorporating meaningful colours and motifs taken from everyday life and mythical creatures, participants crowd the street in a colourful procession accompanied by the music of drums and trumpets. At a nearby field, folk music and elaborately choreographed dances fill the air with joy.

Day 2: Ceremony at the temples Early in the morning, families make their way to ancient Cham temple towers used to worship local Cham deities. While there are towers up and down the coast from Nha Trang to Phan Thiet, the most active towers used for religious purposes are **Po Rome** (in Hau Sanh), **Po Dam** (Tuy Tinh), **Po Sah Inu** (Phan Ri) and **Po Klong Garai** (Phan Rang; p153) in Ninh Thuan and Binh Thuan provinces. Here, Cham priests ritualistically bathe and reclothe images, asking for blessings, good health and abundant harvests, while devotees look on with their own prepared offerings of rice, eggs, whole chickens, fruit and other gifts. The Raglai people join the Cham in traditional dance and music.

Day 3: Ceremony in the villages After a ritual for the god who protects the village, friends and families gather in their villages to share in the bounty and perform their own rituals at home, as well as organise wholesome activities including weaving, sports, traditional games and folk singing and dancing.

ⓘ A Note to Visitors

The temples and shrines of the deities are sacred sites. As a sign of respect, visitors should dress modestly and make space for the families to prepare offerings and perform rituals.

The Cham have a saying, 'Receiving guests is like bringing gold into the house' – so guests are heartily welcomed during the Kate Festival. If invited into a Cham home, it is best to first greet the elders.

Before drinking, we share the first drops with the Earth, the greatest mother of all, and to the creators of all things before us.

■ **Insights from Inra Jaka,** *Cham poet and artist*

25 Easy, Breezy Coastal
DRIVE

DRIVING | OCEAN VIEWS | OUTDOORS

■■■■■ If there's one place on Vietnam's southeastern coast to rent a scooter and enjoy the ride, it's Mui Ne. With just one main road that hugs the beach and little traffic, it's a breeze for even the novice driver to get out and explore the beaches with some fun stops along the way.

🗺 How to

Getting around Many places rent out scooters, either half- or full-day (around 200,000d to 250,000d). Arrange the rental through your hotel for convenient on-site drop-off and pickup. Take a photo of the licence plate, as it's easy to forget which bike is yours when parked.

Safety first While there is relatively little traffic on the main Mui Ne tourist stretch, large buses and minivans share the road – give them a wide berth. There are only a couple of petrol stations in town, so ask your hotel where they are.

Ancient Views

Drive up Ba Nai Hill to the **Po Shanu** Cham towers, a trio of ancient stone monuments built by artisans from the kingdom of Champa in the 9th century. While the towers are nicely maintained (and are popular for wedding photos), the bonus views through the trees over Phan Thiet are excellent. Don't miss the souvenir shop on the way out for handwoven Cham textiles and stone sculptures.

Fishy Business

As Parma is to ham, Phan Thiet is to fish sauce. It's fitting that you'll find Vietnam's first and only **Fish Sauce Museum** here, with 14 exhibition spaces showcasing the history of fish sauce as well as the region, including the large wooden vats used to age the layers of fish and salt.

Dragon Fruit

Drive anywhere outside the main tourist strip, and you'll likely pass rows of cactus-like plants that look like a head of hair gone wild. It's dragon fruit – a raucously pink fruit with green tendrils that resemble dragon scales. Its lightly sweet flesh can be white or dark pink, and tastes somewhere between a kiwi and a pear.

Top left Fairy Stream (p143) **Bottom left** Fish Sauce Museum **Top right** Dragon fruit

Beach Eats

Phan Thiet has a sizeable fishing community. For fresh seafood cooked to order, head to **Bo Ke** (literally 'embankment') – home to a string of family-friendly seafood restaurants where you pick your live seafood from a row of aquariums and have it cooked your way (for example, steamed with beer or lemongrass, or stir-fried with tangy tamarind). For a bit more ambience, hang out at the glam **Pit Stop Food Court** with its authentic international offerings (think Hungarian goulash and fish tacos) and chill vibes (it's one of the best places to view the sunset). There's plenty of outdoor seating throughout the day, and often live music in the evenings.

For a sweet treat with sweeping views over Ong Dia Beach with its interesting rock formations, cool off at one of two **ice-cream trucks** (open afternoons and evenings). Both offer

🚶 Explore Like a Local

Way to the beach Along Nguyen Dinh Chieu, look out for signs on your right facing the seaside, indicating 'hidden' paths to local beaches.

Windmills Drive through a valley of coconut groves and farmlands to Asia's largest wind turbines (bonus: 360-degree views of the coast and mountains).

Mui Ne Beach Hang up a hammock and cool off with a dip at this beach a short drive from the red-sand dunes.

Hom Rom Beach Next to Hon Rom village, this harbour/beach is great for walking. If you go in, be careful of the rip tides.

Happy Ride Glamping Choose between lounging inside a dome with a cold coconut or 'roughing' it for a night under starry skies.

■ Recommended by Angeli Castillo, *Mui Ne resident and creative director at Karma Creatives @acp_86*

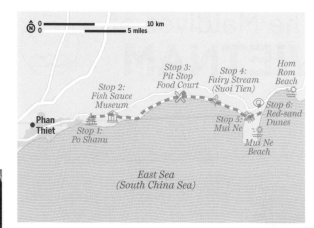

Stop 3: Pit Stop Food Court
Stop 4: Fairy Stream (Suoi Tien)
Hom Rom Beach
Stop 2: Fish Sauce Museum
Stop 6: Red-sand Dunes
Phan Thiet
Stop 1: Po Shanu
Stop 5: Mui Ne
Mui Ne Beach
East Sea (South China Sea)

SOUTHEAST COAST EXPERIENCES

LEFT: HUY THOAI/SHUTTERSTOCK ©; RIGHT: SERINUS/SHUTTERSTOCK ©

Left Beach, Mui Ne Below Sand surfing, Mui Ne

smoothies, drinks and, of course, tropical-flavoured ice cream served in a fresh coconut.

Canyon Walk

The **Fairy Stream (Suoi Tien)** may not be quite as magical as its name implies, but wading the creek's reddish waters past small Grand Canyon–like cliffs makes for a fun outing nonetheless. Clay and limestone create interesting colour striations in the rock, contrasted on the other side with forest green.

Fishing Fleet

With all the hotels and restaurants on the main tourist strip, it's hard to believe this area was once a simple **fishing village**. But just beyond the strip, you can see there's still a vibrant fishing industry here. 'Mui Ne' means 'Cape of Escape' – a place where boats would harbour in bad weather. Arrive early in the morning to see the boats bringing in the night's catch to women waiting on the beach to sort and prepare the fish for the market.

Sand Play

It's strange to think that a tropical country like Vietnam might have desert-like sand dunes, but that alternate reality exists in Mui Ne. Closer to town, you'll find the **red-sand dunes**, where you can rent plastic mats to slide down the hills. The more impressive white-sand dunes are 24km northeast of town, with ATVs and dune buggies for rent.

26

The Maldives of
VIETNAM

BEACHES | RUINS | SEAFOOD

Situated between the tourist hotspots of Hoi An and Nha Trang, coastal Quy Nhon has all the makings of an excellent beach getaway minus the crowds. True travel insiders know to visit this laid-back town – with easy access, fresh seafood, and 45km of coastline boasting some of Vietnam's most dramatic beaches – sooner rather than later.

🗺 **How to**

Getting there Phu Cat Airport serves Quy Nhon and taxis and shuttle buses make the 35km trip into town. It's also on the north–south railway line in between Danang and Nha Trang, including the option to travel aboard the luxe *Vietage* carriage to/from Danang.

When to go January to August sees sunny weather with little rain. Seasonal storms and rough seas from September to December may suspend boat trips.

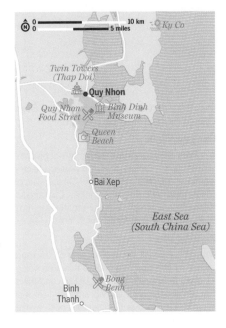

Ancient arts Part of the area occupied by the seafaring Champa civilisation, Quy Nhon has several ancient sites, including the red-brick **Twin Towers (Thap Doi)** from the late 12th century, which are some of the country's best preserved. The more scenic **Banh It** towers are 15km northwest of the city. For a fine collection of Cham sculptures, head to the **Binh Dinh Museum**, also home to an impressive display of performance masks used in traditional Vietnamese opera.

Beaches and islands Calling **Ky Co** the 'Maldives of Vietnam' may be a stretch, but

Top right Eo Gio **Bottom right** Twin Towers (Thap Doi)

✂ Dining on Water

Head south to the floating restaurants at **Bong Benh** and enjoy great views of colourful fishing boats while you wait for the kitchen to cook up fresh seafood to order.

Quy Nhon's premier beach attraction is certainly beautiful – a lovely bay of crystalline waters backed by green mountains. It's accessible by a challenging motorbike ride or boat tours combining Ky Co and nearby **Eo Gio**, where walkways lead down to interesting rock formations and sweeping views. Quy Nhon also has a very clean city beach with golden sand and a park-like boardwalk; nearby **Queen Beach** is a favourite photo spot, more for its smooth boulders (which is why locals call it 'Egg Beach') than for swimming. Offshore, uninhabited **Hon Kho** or the more developed **Cu Lao Xanh** make for nice day trips.

Beach eats Quy Nhon specialities include *tre* (fermented pig's ear flavoured with sesame and galangal) and *banh xeo tom nhay*, a savoury rice-flour crêpe loaded with shrimp and wrapped up in rice paper with shredded mango and fresh herbs. Head to the evening **Quy Nhon Food Street** on Ngo Van So and chow down on many of the region's best-loved eats.

City-Beach
GETAWAY

BEACHES | VIEWS | SEAFOOD

Just about two hours from Ho Chi Minh City, Vung Tau is the closest beach destination from the city. While its beaches aren't as pretty as the islands or those along the southeastern coast, the salty air, fresh seafood and easy access make a trip to Vung Tau a nice change of pace, especially if you have more than a few days in HCMC.

How to

Getting there A range of options makes it easy to get to Vung Tau, including ferry, private bus and cars for hire. However, the minibus is both comfortable and can drop you off right at your hotel.

Avoid tourist traps Vung Tau gets particularly crowded on weekends and holidays, and while the seafood restaurants are a highlight, remember to check your bill carefully as places have been known to overcharge tourists.

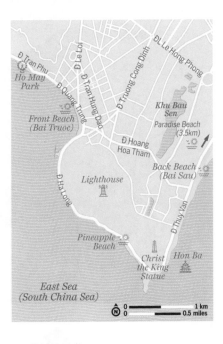

Beaches Among Vung Tau's public city beaches, **Front Beach (Bai Truoc)** is busiest with its many hotels and restaurants, and is also the jumping-off point for the cable car. **Back Beach (Bai Sau)** is cleaner, preferred by locals, and even has some surfing (around November and December). For something quieter, head to rocky **Pineapple Beach (Bai Dua)** or pay an entrance fee to enjoy the amenities at **Paradise Beach**.

Sea views The hills around Vung Tau offer gorgeous views of the city and the sea. Climb more than 800 steps to the giant **Christ the King** statue

Top right Coastal road, Vung Tau
Bottom right Hon Ba

CRAVENA/SHUTTERSTOCK ©

MILA DEMIDOVA/SHUTTERSTOCK ©

Secluded Beaches

Leave the crowds behind at the less developed beaches just northeast of Vung Tau, including **Long Hai**, **Ho Tram** and **Ho Coc**, known for their wild, secluded vibes.

atop Small Mountain. At 32m tall, it's just short of its Brazilian counterpart and offers exceptional views, especially if you navigate the spiral staircase up to the vantage point on the statue's shoulders. Some prefer the more open views from the base of the Vung Tau **lighthouse**, built by the French in 1862 on the other side of the mountain. Grab a chilled homemade yogurt or a soft-boiled egg as a treat at **Co Tien** as you exit. The easiest way to enjoy the view is from the cable car going up to **Ho May Park**. The return ticket includes entrance to the amusement park, with a range of rides and cultural shows.

Temple trekking The island temple of **Hon Ba** can only be accessed on foot once a month (around the 14th or 15th of each lunar month), when a slippery, rocky 200m path is exposed at low tide. This small temple from 1881 is dedicated to a female deity believed to protect locals from natural disasters; there's even an underground meeting room, used during wartime.

28 Serene Marine **LIFE**

BEACHES | HIKING | DIVING

With little nightlife to speak of, Con Dao is all about getting back to nature. Thankfully, this gorgeous island is packed with outdoor adventures, including hiking in the national park, driving along the coastal road with mountains on one side and the deep blue sea on the other, and diving and snorkelling in the crystalline waters inhabited by dugongs, dolphins and sea turtles.

KERNELNGUYEN/SHUTTERSTOCK ©

📖 How to

Getting here There are ferries from Soc Trang (three hours) and Vung Tau (12 hours), but a 45-minute flight from Ho Chi Minh City is far more comfortable.

When to go The dry season is December to April; the turtle-nesting season is June to September. In the wet season, monsoon rains may affect the ferries and water activities. Diving and snorkelling is best from February to July.

Scooting around With one main road, it's impossible to get lost. Even novice drivers will enjoy cruising the island on a motor scooter.

TAPPASAN PHURISAMRIT/SHUTTERSTOCK ©

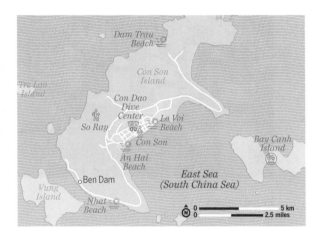

Top left Mountain scenery, Con Dao
Bottom left Nhat Beach

Hiking Con Dao National Park covers 80% of the island, so hiking is a great way to explore. Stop by the park office and pick up a map of the trails or book a hiking tour led by a ranger, from an easy 2km walk to a strenuous 16km challenge. One of the easier trails leads up to **So Ray**, a fruit plantation where prisoners worked, with pretty town views.

Walking The main town of **Con Son** is easily walkable, with attractions close together including the prisons, museums and French-era buildings. The market is a nice place to pick up a bag of Con Dao almonds. Along the promenade by Pier 914 (named after the number of prisoners who died in its construction) are cafes with beautiful views out to sea and maybe even a game of beach football.

Beach-hopping Hop on a scooter to explore the island's beaches, starting with **Dam Trau Beach** in the northwest. Shaded by casuarina trees, this golden-sand beach with glassy, calm water is perhaps the island's best. Closer to town is **Lo Voi Beach**, great for walking; **An Hai Beach** starts in town and stretches southward. Just past Shark Cape at the island's southern end, **Nhat Beach** is revealed only during low tide.

Island-hopping Con Dao has some of Vietnam's best diving and snorkelling. Boat trips to the nearby islands can be arranged through hotels, **Con Dao Dive Center** (p152) or the national park. If you're on Con Dao between June and September, the park organises overnight trips to **Bay Canh Island**, where you may see the turtles laying their eggs.

🐟 Diving Con Dao

Con Dao has over 400 species of corals, including some of the best hard corals in the world like staghorn, table and boulder coral. The waters around Con Dao are also home to dugongs, turtles, whale sharks, barracuda and batfish, as well as a vast range of colourful reef fish. There are over 25 dive sites around Con Dao catering to everyone from complete beginners (making it a good place to do a try drive, with no prior experience necessary) to very experienced divers. The only time to go diving in Con Dao is from February to October. There is no diving from November to January due to high winds, high swells and very poor visibility.

■ **Insights from Daniel Coldrey,** owner of Con Dao Dive Center @condaodivecenter

Paradise with a Past

OVERCOMING CON DAO'S DARK HISTORY

Just 80km off Vietnam's southern coast, the Con Dao archipelago is best known to the Vietnamese as a pilgrimage site. However, with crystal-clear water, lush forests and the chilliest of vibes, it's just a matter of time until Con Dao goes from insider secret to mainstream hotspot.

Left Hang Duong Cemetery
Middle Con Dao Prison Museum
Right Vo Thi Sau's gravesite

PETER STUCKINGS/SHUTTERSTOCK ©

Penal Colony

Ask any Vietnamese about Con Dao and it's likely not windswept beaches and jungle-clad hillsides that come to mind. Instead, it's the names of countless national heroes who were imprisoned there during the 113 years the island was used as a penal colony, first under French and then South Vietnamese rule.

With its remote location and natural defences, Con Dao has long been the unfortunate home for many of Vietnam's resistance figures, starting with Lady Phi Yen. In the late 18th century, the wife of Nguyen Emperor Gia Long was banished there for objecting to her husband's call for assistance from the French to quash a civil war.

Later, under French control, the island was home to the largest prison complex in all of Indochina, housing tens of thousands of prisoners in terrible conditions, giving rise to its designation as 'hell on earth'.

Vo Thi Sau

Out of all the people who passed through Con Dao's atrocious penal system, its most famous resident is Vo Thi Sau, a teenage resistance fighter brought to Con Dao and executed in 1952 for throwing a bomb into a patrol of French soldiers.

For the Vietnamese, a trip to Con Dao is about paying respects to this brave teen, often flying in for just a day to visit her memorial museum where glass cases are full of gifts like lipstick and hair clips – accessories for a girl who will forever remain 19. At the Hang Duong Cemetery, just

past Con Son's central market, crowds bearing fresh flowers, paper money and bags of fruit gather for evening vigils at Vo Thi Sau's gravesite. She and her fallen comrades have become guardian angels of the island, known as 'the Altar of Vietnam'. It's believed to be an intensely spiritual place, where personal prayers are asked and answered.

Island of Heroes

'Con Dao is an island of heroes, a great historical monument' – this is what, according to a plaque in the Con Dao Museum, General Secretary Le Duan declared on visiting the island in 1976, a year after the prisons were closed. Of the 7448 freed prisoners, 157 chose to stay behind, later joined by volunteers from the mainland willing to weather the spartan conditions to create a new life for themselves. 'Relatives who relocated before us said life was peaceful here with nothing but clouds, sky, water and mountains. It was very wild at the time – only about 1200 residents and 1000 or so soldiers', remembers Minh who came to Con Dao in the early 1980s from the Mekong Delta.

> Vo Thi Sau and her fallen comrades have become guardian angels of the island, known as 'the Altar of Vietnam'.

Today, Con Dao has a population of about 10,500, a third of whom are military personnel. Where the water and forests were once jailers used to keep people from leaving, they now beckon travellers looking for a quiet paradise, albeit one with a hellish past.

🏛 Getting to Know the Island

The spacious, modern **Con Dao Museum** makes for an excellent introduction to the island. Spread over 1700 sq metres of exhibition space, there are four main areas of focus showcasing more than 2000 items, but visitors will likely gravitate to displays on the island's natural resources (including a preserved dugong) and its history as a penal colony. Note the dioramas recreating life inside the prisons, the shrine-like area dedicated to Vo Thi Sau, and the objects made by the resourceful prisoners over the years, from embroidered handkerchiefs to makeshift goggles.

Listings

BEST OF THE REST

 See & Do

Funky Monkey

One-stop shop for island tours off the coast of Nha Trang. In addition to the ubiquitous four-island tour, they also do trips to some of the lesser-known but stunningly beautiful islands like Hon Noi, Diep Son, Doc Let and Binh Hung.

Rainbow Divers

Since 1996, Rainbow Divers has been offering diving and snorkelling in Nha Trang, its flagship location. If you're looking to get PADI training, Nha Trang offers excellent value. Lots of daily dive options including try dives.

Con Dao Dive Center

The only dive centre permanently based on Con Dao, this is the place to go to explore the 25 dive sites spread across three islands. There are also courses for PADI, EFR and Rescue Diving.

Imperial Beach Club

Enjoy a day at the beach in style with a day pass from the Imperial Beach Club on Vung Tau's Back Beach. Inspired by Roman baths, it has a large pool and plenty of loungers. Private air-conditioned cabanas are also available.

Van Thuy Tu Temple

Built in 1762 in Phan Thiet, this small temple celebrates whales, believed to protect local fishers from bad weather and dangers at sea. The star attraction is a 22m-long whale skeleton. There's even a biennial whale-worshipping festival in early September.

VinWonders Nha Trang

Take the 3300m-long cable car to Bamboo Island and spend the day at VinWonders, a giant amusement park with a 120m-high Ferris wheel, water park, aquarium, zoo, mountain slide, live performances and more.

 Get Healthy

Thap Ba Hot Springs

At the original mud-bath centre in Nha Trang, prepare to get dirty with a soak in a slippery mineral-mud bath, followed by a dip in the heated mineral-water swimming pool. Herbal baths and massage treatments are also available.

Minera Hot Springs Binh Chau

About an hour and a half from Vung Tau, Minera is home to Southeast Asia's largest outdoor mineral-water pool. There's also a Japanese-style onsen and a spa area inspired by other countries (think Turkish baths and wine baths).

 Beach Eats

Quan Nem Nuong Dang Van Quyen $

Nha Trang's non-seafood speciality is *nem nuong Ninh Hoa,* and this eatery is the city's most popular for its juicy grilled pork, crunchy

Van Thuy Tu Temple

rice paper and thick dipping sauce. There are two locations but the original is near Dam Market.

Banh Khot Ba Hai $

A few blocks back from Vung Tau's Front Beach, this local fave gets high marks for crispy-but-not-oily rice cakes topped with shrimp.

Cafe Con Son $

Right across from Pier 914 on Con Dao, this no-frills cafe serves up coffee, juice and shakes with great sea views.

B&B Cafe $

On the grounds of Ca Ty Resort, this spacious Phan Thiet cafe has lots of seating and beach access. Bring a towel and spend the day sipping value-priced sodas and coconut coffees.

Cham Connection

Po Klong Garai Cham Towers

This Hindu Cham religious complex of three towers, 6km west of Phan Rang, was built in the late 13th to early 14th centuries. Its well-preserved main tower is viewed as one of the most impressive anywhere in Vietnam.

Lang Nghe Det Tho Cam Cham

Watch artisans working over traditional Cham looms, weaving beautiful scarves and other textiles that incorporate age-old motifs, at this village collective 20 minutes south of Phan Rang.

Cham Cultural Centre

In My Nghiep weaving village outside Phan Rang, this exhibition space owned by Mrs Inrahani showcases Cham culture through a collection of books in the Cham language, a display of Cham artefacts, and women weaving textiles using traditional looms.

Po Klong Garai Cham Towers

 ## Sea-to-Table Dining

Hai San Ben Cang Nha Trang $$

This eatery 10 minutes southwest of Nha Trang's city beach gets rave reviews from locals for its wide selection of live seafood at reasonable prices.

BiBo Quan $$

Right on the Mui Ne strip, spacious BiBo Quan is popular with Vietnamese tourists for its friendly service and super-fresh seafood at wallet-friendly prices.

Banh Xeo Tom Nhay Gia Vy $

With two locations, this long-time Quy Nhon favourite serves up crispy Vietnamese crêpes loaded with shrimp, beef, egg or vegetables. Rolled up in rice paper with fresh veggies, one is a snack while two make a delicious meal.

Sandals Kitchen & Bar $$$

Good food packed with flavour and beautifully presented makes beach-chic Sandals a winner, even if you aren't staying at the Sailing Club Mui Ne. The prawn tacos and green-tea-roasted, locally sourced black kingfish are delightful.

 Scan to find more things to do on the Southeast Coast online

THE HIGHLANDS

NATURE | ADVENTURE | ETHNIC GROUPS

Experi-
ence the
Highlands
online

THE HIGHLANDS
Trip Builder

The central highlands offer a cool respite from Vietnam's heat and humidity. Immerse yourself in coffee and culture in off-the-beaten-path Buon Ma Thuot, or explore Dalat – built as a wellness hill station by the French – with its beautiful mountains and lakes.

Visit the **World of Coffee Museum** in Buon Ma Thuot, Vietnam's coffee capital (p171)

🚗 7min from the city centre

Buon Don

Serepok River

Yok Don National Park

Ea T'Ling

Buon Ma Thuot

Dak Mil

CAMBODIA

Ea Krong

Learn all about how coffee is grown and processed at **K'Ho Coffee Farm** (p168)

🚗 30min from Dalat Market

Gia Nghia

Dang Boa

Sample a **Dalat pizza**, grilled rice paper with oddly wonderful toppings (p159), in the centre of Dalat.
City centre

Phuoc Long

Binh Long

Nghia Thanh

Di Linh

Bao Loc

Dong Xoai

Cat Tien National Park

Chon Thanh

Da M'Ri

Bau Tong

Ma Da Gui

Phu Lam

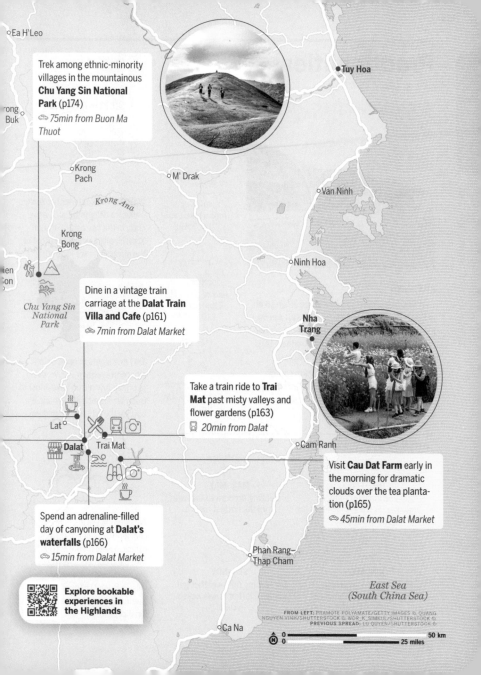

○ Ea H'Leo

Trek among ethnic-minority villages in the mountainous **Chu Yang Sin National Park** (p174)
🚌 *75min from Buon Ma Thuot*

● Tuy Hoa

rong
Buk

○ Krong Pach

○ M' Drak

○ Van Ninh

Krong Ana

Krong Bong

○ Ninh Hoa

ien
on

Chu Yang Sin National Park

Dine in a vintage train carriage at the **Dalat Train Villa and Cafe** (p161)
🚌 *7min from Dalat Market*

Nha Trang

Lat ○

Take a train ride to **Trai Mat** past misty valleys and flower gardens (p163)
🚆 *20min from Dalat*

Dalat Trai Mat

○ Cam Ranh

Visit **Cau Dat Farm** early in the morning for dramatic clouds over the tea plantation (p165)
🚌 *45min from Dalat Market*

Spend an adrenaline-filled day of canyoning at **Dalat's waterfalls** (p166)
🚌 *15min from Dalat Market*

Phan Rang–
Thap Cham

*East Sea
(South China Sea)*

Explore bookable experiences in the Highlands

FROM LEFT: PRAMOTE POLYAMATE/GETTY IMAGES ©, QUANG NGUYEN VINH/SHUTTERSTOCK ©, WOR_K_SIMKUL/SHUTTERSTOCK ©, PREVIOUS SPREAD: LU QUYEN/SHUTTERSTOCK ©

○ Ca Na

0   50 km
0   25 miles

Practicalities

ARRIVING

Lien Khuong Airport Located about 30km south of Dalat. There's a shuttle bus (40,000d) and metered taxis to town. The long-distance bus station is just 1.5km from the city centre. Fixed-fare taxis can be prearranged to and from the airport.

Buon Ma Thuot Airport Located 8km east of town; the bus station is 4km northeast of the city centre. Catch a metered taxi right outside the airport.

HOW MUCH FOR A

full-day
motorbike tour
700,000d

kilo of Buon Ma
Thuot coffee
130,000d

return train from
Dalat to Trai Mat
108,000d

GETTING AROUND

Walking The cool weather makes walking a delight in Dalat, especially in the city centre around Xuan Huong Lake where most of the attractions are located.

Taxi Any sights outside Dalat's city centre require a drive, even to pretty Tuyen Lam Lake. Most of Buon Ma Thuot's attractions are outside the city centre, making taxis or tours a must.

Two wheels Dalat's hilly terrain is best left to confident drivers, especially the mountain roads with blind corners. Cycling is pleasant, but be prepared for hills. In Buon Ma Thuot, *xe om* (motorbike taxis) are easy to find for short trips.

WHEN TO GO

DEC–FEB
Cool and ideal for outdoor activities. Festival season in Buon Ma Thuot.

MAR–MAY
Increasing amount of rain with April the hottest month.

JUN–AUG
Rainy season, with high humidity. Peak for domestic travel in Dalat.

SEP–NOV
Decreasing rain, weather gets cooler. Start of flower season in Dalat.

EATING & DRINKING

Dalat has few specialities other than artichoke soup cooked with ham hocks and the Dalat 'pizza' (pictured top right), grilled rice paper topped with a hodgepodge of ingredients like dried shrimp, egg and scallions. Food simply tastes better here because of the incredibly fresh ingredients grown locally, such as bell peppers, cauliflower, artichokes and strawberries. In Buon Ma Thuot, try the a and *bun do* (hearty soup with thick rice noodles in a broth of simmering pork bones and crab meat).

Best bun do

Quan Thu (p175)

Must-try Dalat pizza

Banh Trang Nuong Be Lun (p175)

WHERE TO STAY

Dalat has a wide range of accommodation options, from camping to mini-hotels to five-star accommodation by the lake. Buon Ma Thuot has a much smaller selection.

CONNECT & FIND YOUR WAY

Wi-fi Coverage is good in urban areas, but remember that in the central highlands most attractions are located away from the cities – in mountains, valleys and deep into national parks. If internet connection is important to you, it's best to secure a data plan.

Navigation While most attractions are signposted, Google Maps is helpful for off-the-beaten-path locations.

Place	Pro/Con
Buon Ma Thuot	For convenience, stay near the main market, but most attractions are outside the city.
Dalat city centre	Easy walking distance to many restaurants, shopping venues and attractions. Traffic and noise can be an issue.
Tuyen Lam Lake	Gorgeous lakeside resorts with beautiful views and access to outdoor activities. Inconvenient for frequent trips to the city centre.
French Quarter	Refurbished colonial-era villas are perfect for a romantic, quiet setting, though rooms can feel worn.

MONEY

Because Buon Ma Thuot isn't yet on the tourist trail, expect accommodation to cost slightly more than comparable properties elsewhere. In Dalat, skip the taxis for short distances and enjoy longer walks instead.

TRY HOMESTAYS

Many homestays in the highlands are delightfully charming with beautiful, natural surroundings (Dalat) or providing the opportunity to interact with ethnic-minority families (Buon Ma Thuot).

GODONG/GETTY IMAGES ©

A Corner of Europe in Vietnam

DALAT'S FOUNDING AS A HILL-STATION RETREAT

There's nowhere in Vietnam quite like Dalat, which feels more like Europe than Asia. There's nippy mountain air, luscious strawberries and giant artichokes neatly arranged at the local market, and houses looking like they were plucked from the French countryside. It almost feels too good to be real.

Left Dalat Palace Heritage Hotel
Middle Dalat Train Villa and Cafe
Right Flowers, Dalat

By the 19th century, France had thriving colonies across the globe in Europe, North Africa and the Caribbean. However, Cochinchina (as southern Vietnam was then called) was a different story. Death and disease were ever-present, exacerbated by the stifling heat, making it one of the most dangerous places to be a colonist. An 1892 report commented that people might die within six months, despite the quality of the soil and the abundance of water.

In those days, the only choices for an ill colonist needing a life-saving change of scenery were a 12-day journey to the French wellness centre in Yokohama, Japan, or an even longer, deadlier ocean crossing back to France.

So began an extensive search for a suitable location right in Cochinchina to build a wellness retreat, somewhere the colonists could find themselves transported back to a Mediterranean-like environment with cool temperatures and secluded altitude much like the British had established in Darjeeling (India) and the Dutch in Bogor (Indonesia).

Dr Alexandre Yersin (one of the discoverers of the bubonic-plague bacillus) is credited for recommending the Lang Bian plateau in 1893 as the site for a purpose-built hill station to accommodate suffering French colonists, given that it was within hours from Saigon by train and that the climate was similar to that of France.

Thus began the inhuman task of transforming the site, then inhabited by the K'Ho ethnic group, into a corner of France. Over the next three decades, thousands of porters

(including Vietnamese, hill-tribes people who were thought of as easier to control, and even convicts) were conscripted into bringing supplies up the mountain. One source estimated that by 1908, at least 20,000 workers had died in the effort to build Dalat and connect it to the outside world.

Due to steep gradients and a remote location, it took nearly 30 years to complete a railway between Dalat and Phan Rang on the coast to ferry passengers to this idyllic world of game hunting, rowing parties and tennis tournaments. Dalat's popularity as a cool retreat surged with each world war – it was a much more palatable holiday destination without dangerous sailings back to Europe where U-boats and other perils awaited.

> By 1908, at least 20,000 workers had died in the effort to build Dalat and connect it to the outside world.

Sick of canned goods and local fare, the French also experimented with growing fruits and vegetables that reminded them of home, including artichokes, Brussels sprouts, strawberries and grapes. Even today, Dalat farmers continue to experiment with growing foodstuffss that can't be found in any other region in Vietnam, like rhubarb, microgreens and edible flowers.

With its faded colonial-era villas, artificial lakes surrounded by pine trees, and greenhouses growing flowers and cool-weather vegetables, it doesn't take much to envision Dalat in its heyday – a corner of Europe in Vietnam.

🏛 Turn Back Time

If you want to experience what the high life must have been like in early Dalat, visit the **Dalat Palace Heritage Hotel,** which opened in 1922. The rooms feature ornate period furnishings, chandeliers, a cast-iron bathtub and a working fireplace, spread over 5 hectares of forested grounds right in town. To stay in a fully restored villa from the 1920s and '30s, head to the **Ana Mandara Villas Dalat Resort & Spa** where upgrades have aimed to keep as much of the original character as possible, including stone paths and painted tiles. Just up the hill from the city's art-deco train station, the **Dalat Train Villa and Cafe** serves up value-priced meals in a meticulously restored train carriage from 1910.

29 A Day
IN DALAT

TRAIN | HIGH TEA | MARKET EATS

███████ Spend a delightful day exploring Dalat, the 'City of Eternal Spring'. Year-round pleasant temperatures and fresh air fuel long walks around the lake and past colonial-era buildings with forays into the surrounding valleys where fruit and flowers are grown.

WITHGOD/SHUTTERSTOCK ©

🗺 Trip Notes

Getting here Dalat is served by Lien Khuong Airport, 30km south of town. Shuttles and fixed-rate taxis make the trip between the two. The city is also well served by buses, including overnight trips from Ho Chi Minh City.

Where to stay First-timers to Dalat should stay close to the city centre, where most of the attractions are located. If staying longer, consider spending a couple of nights by gorgeous Tuyen Lam Lake.

When to go Try to avoid Dalat between June and August as places get crowded fast, taking away most of Dalat's charms.

ⓘ Civet Coffee

Civet (or weasel) coffee is sometimes on the menu, brewed from beans that have been digested by a catlike creature, supposedly resulting in a smoother cup of coffee. Wild civets are often kept in poor, cramped conditions, leading many informed travellers to avoid supporting this ethically questionable product.

01 Start the day like a local with a brisk walk around **Xuan Huong Lake**, stopping for a swan-boat ride, a visit to the city flower garden, or a coffee overlooking the water.

05 Grab a seat on the stairs at the **Central Market** (pictured opposite) and chow down on a Dalat 'pizza' with eclectic toppings like egg, cheese, beef and mayonnaise over grilled rice paper.

02 Board the train at the art-deco railway station and enjoy the 7km ride to **Trai Mat** past misty valleys. Explore the pretty Linh Phuoc Pagoda covered in stunning mosaics.

03 Opened in 1922, the **Dalat Palace Heritage Hotel** attracted the *crème de la crème* of visitors. Sit down for high tea in the elegant Le Rabelais, reminiscent of a French salon.

04 Completed in 1942 by the French, the impressive **St Nicholas Cathedral** has a 47m-high bell tower topped by a weathercock – hence the nickname 'Chicken Church'.

500 m
0.25 miles

Đ Tran Quoc Toan

Golf Course

Đ Dinh Tien Hoang

Đ Bui Thi Xuan

Đ Tran Quoc Toan

Trai Mat (7km)

Đ Nguyen Trai

Xuan Huong Lake

Đ Tran Quoc Toan

Đ Yersin

Đ Tran Phu

30 Picture **PERFECT**

PHOTOGRAPHY | FLOWERS | HERITAGE BUILDINGS

▬▬▬ From misty valleys and cloud-covered mountains to fields of flowers and French colonial-era buildings (both crumbling and restored), Dalat is truly a photographer's paradise. Go out in search of the perfect backdrop for that envy-inducing selfie while exploring Dalat's beautiful landscapes.

WOR_K_SIMEUL/SHUTTERSTOCK ©

🗺 How to

Getting there Arrange a taxi if it's off the beaten path, making sure the driver knows where to go.

When to go Many of these spots are best shot very early in the morning.

Etiquette While there's no shortage of fee-paying spots designed specifically for taking photos, the greenhouses and farms are private property. That said, most locals will allow you to wander as long as you're careful where you step and respect that these are active workplaces.

NGUYEN NGUYEN/SHUTTERSTOCK ©

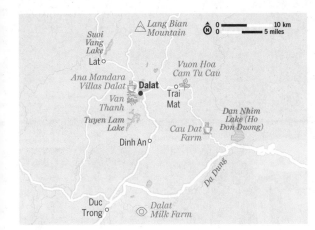

Top left Flower field, Trai Mat **Bottom left** Cau Dat Farm

📷 Dalat Photography Tips

Prepare to arrive early to capture beautiful sunrises. Better yet, camp where you want to shoot and start taking photos with the sun.

Don't forget to include yourself in your landscape shots. Ask a friend or bring a tripod.

Play around with natural lighting. For contrast, try putting your subject half in and half out of the sunlight.

Dalat is ideal for flower photography. Try close-up shots to capture the vibrant colours.

The people of Dalat are very friendly and will often allow you to take portrait shots – just ask politely and with a smile.

■ **Insights from Tran Ngoc,** *creative director at Centro Vietnam @ngoctran_ photographer*

Cloud hunting From early morning mist that settles in the valleys to clouds hanging below mountain peaks, Mother Nature provides the drama. Take the first train to **Trai Mat** to capture fields of fruit and flowers shrouded by mist, with a stop at **Vuon Hoa Cam Tu Cau** for the nearby hydrangea fields. For views from up high, climb up **Lang Biang Mountain** or head 23km southeast of Dalat to **Cau Dat Farm**, where you can photograph the clouds hanging over the nearly 100-year-old tea plantation while sipping a cup of oolong cold brew.

The French factor While the whole town has a distinctly European feel, the **French Quarter** on Đ Tran Hung Dao has the highest concentration of colonial-era summer homes. A few are abandoned but many have been repurposed into quaint cafes or guesthouses. Otherwise, go for high tea at the fully restored **Ana Mandara Villas Dalat** and find the perfect corner among the ivy-covered walls, pretty flower gardens and two 1930s Citroën convertibles.

Flower power More than 90 sq km around Dalat produce over 3 billion flower branches, making Dalat Vietnam's flower capital. Just 3km from the town centre is the flower village of **Van Thanh**. Ask nicely to enter the greenhouses filled with roses, carnations, daisies and more. Alternatively, head 35km south of Dalat to **Dalat Milk Farm**, 68 sq km of farmland filled with fields of wildflowers, sunflowers, pine-tree-lined paths and quaint European-style buildings.

31

The Great
OUTDOORS

HIKING | CANYONING | BIKING

▬▬▬ Blessed with waterfalls, lakes, mountains and forests, the Dalat region is tailor-made for outdoor adventures, with most activities just minutes from the city centre. Swim under the waterfalls, hike up majestic peaks or enjoy a leisurely picnic by the lake – there are plenty of options for reconnecting with nature.

Top left Truc Lam Pagoda (p169) **Bottom right** Bidoup Nui Ba National Park (p169) **Top right** Tuyem Lam Lake (p169)

🗺 How to

Getting here/around
Most hotels can help arrange bicycle or motorbike rentals. Due to the curvy mountain roads, driving a motorbike here is best left to experienced drivers.

When to go Dalat's altitude means pleasant weather year-round; however, November to March is the dry season. During this time, temperatures can go as low as 20°C, which is great for outdoor activities, but you should pack a jacket for the cooler evenings.

Local insight Tap into local knowledge with Facebook groups 'Dalat Today' and 'Expats in Dalat'.

Fantastic Falls

Dalat has an abundance of waterfalls, both to admire and for swimming. One of the most magnificent is the 30m-high **Elephant Falls**, about 45 minutes outside the city. Carefully navigate the steep, slippery path down and you'll be rewarded with views looking up at the fast-flowing waterfall with a bonus cave to explore. Bring a tent and stay at the nearby **Lieng Rowoa Camp** (p175) for an extra dose of nature.

The largest waterfall in the area is **Pongour**, just south of the Lien Khuong Airport. A popular picnic spot, the seven tiers of these 100m-wide falls are most impressive during the rainy season from July to October. **Ankroet**, Vietnam's first hydropower plant (which was built in the 1940s), is more of a stream

🚆 Trainspotting

Railway enthusiasts can find fascinating remnants of the now defunct **Dalat–Thap Cham Cog Railway** from the French colonial era. From the Dalat Train Station, take Hwy 20 towards Thap Cham; the abandoned Da Tho train station is at Km 12.1, Tunnel 5 at Km 15.7, and Tunnel 4 at Km 17.3.

■ **Recommended by Curtis King,** *owner of Dalat Train Cafe*
@dalattrainvillacafe

that tumbles over rocks than a waterfall. That said, the surrounding pine forests and gentle cascades offer a pleasant spot to picnic.

Mountain Biking

Dalat's hilly terrain with pine forests (not jungle), together with its cool weather, make it an ideal destination for mountain biking. Lots of places rent bicycles, but you'll need to tap one of the adventure tour operators to rent a true mountain bike. Unofficial trails used by locals can be connected to create 30km to 40km routes through forests and past vegetable farms and coffee plantations.

Coffee Culture

While most of Vietnam produces robusta, Dalat's altitude allows growing the more highly prized arabica beans, often cultivated by members of the K'Ho minority group, the first growers of coffee in the region. Stop by **K'Ho Coffee Farm**, a cooperative of about 50

🧗 Adrenaline Junkies

A great way to explore Dalat's natural scenery is by canyoning; it's one of the only places in Vietnam to try this thrilling sport. All canyoning trips organised by official operators start from **Datanla Falls**, 5km from the city centre, and require an additional 4km walk along uneven, slippery terrain. However, good swimmers comfortable with heights are in for an adrenaline-filled day of abseiling, scrambling and sliding down rock faces, and cliff jumping from a height of 6m to 10m. A dam upstream controls the water, meaning canyoning is possible year-round. There is some risk involved, so be sure to book with a trained and certified tour provider.

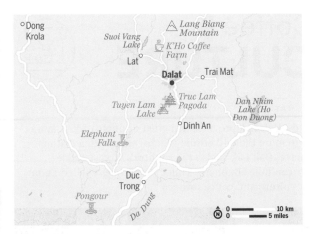

Left Canyoning, Datanla Falls
Below Pongour (p167)

K'Ho families growing arabica coffee on Lang Bian Mountain, for a half-day workshop starting with a walk through the organic farm to learn about the entire process including fermentation and roasting, finishing up with lunch and, of course, a cup of freshly brewed coffee.

Lake Views

The beautiful 350-hectare **Tuyen Lam Lake**, 6km south of Dalat, is surrounded by pine forests and makes for a great outing. Take the 2.3km cable car to **Truc Lam Pagoda**, walk to the lake and go boating, camping, hiking up to **Pinhat Peak** or trekking through the pine forests.

Mountain Highs

Designated a Unesco Biosphere Reserve in 2015, **Lang Biang** (including Bidoup Nui Ba National Park) is home to more than 2000 plant species and approximately 400 animal species, including more than a hundred rare species on Vietnam's red list. Hike two to three hours along a steep dirt path to the 2167m-high **Lang Biang Peak** or take a vintage Russian 4WD to the (slightly lower) former American radar base, both offering sweeping views of the town, river and valleys below. On some evenings, there's a show at the mountain base involving traditional K'Ho dances, gongs, rice wine and a bonfire.

32 Coffee & **CULTURE**

COFFEE | ETHNIC GROUPS | NATURE

The central highlands' Dak Lak province is a great example of Vietnam's ethnic diversity. It's home to more than 40 ethnic groups, each with a distinct culture, religion and language. Dak Lak is also the country's largest coffee-growing region, making its capital of Buon Ma Thuot (sometimes spelled Buon Me Thuot) a must-visit for culture and coffee lovers.

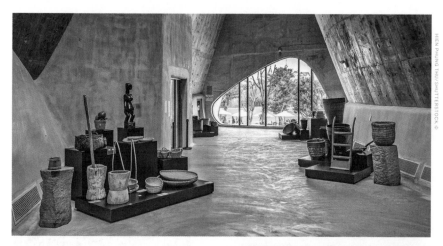

HIEN PHUNG THU/SHUTTERSTOCK ©

📷 How to

Getting here/around Buon Ma Thuot Airport is 8km east of town, with domestic flights from major cities. Attractions are spread out, so it's best to hire a motorbike or book tours.

When to go The rainy season is May to October, resulting in lush scenery but muddy roads. The dry season is November to April. March sees two biennial events, the Buon Don Ethnic Traditional Cultural Festival and the Buon Ma Thuot Coffee Festival.

Buying coffee Stock up on coffee here to get the real thing at lower prices than in major cities.

DORSTEFFEN/SHUTTERSTOCK ©

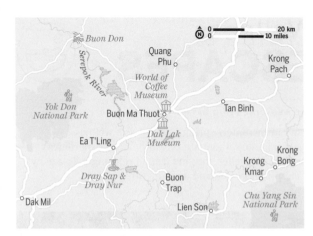

Top left World of Coffee Museum
Bottom left Elephant, Yok Don National Park

The excellent **Dak Lak Museum** has over 10,000 artefacts showcasing the history, biodiversity and culture of the many ethnic groups living in the region. To visit minority groups, head 40km northwest to **Buon Don**, an Ede village once famous for elephant hunting and taming. While the village has thankfully transitioned away from elephant rides and performances, there are guided tours of traditional longhouses, music and dance performances, and walks through the forest.

Just across the river is the 1150-sq-km **Yok Don National Park**, home to 89 species of mammals including wild elephants, water buffalo and gaurs, as well as 305 species of birds and 48 species of reptiles. The park organises guided walks, trekking, birdwatching, fishing and other activities. Another popular natural attraction is the **Dray Sap** and **Dray Nur** waterfalls (known in Vietnamese as the 'Husband and Wife' falls), 25km southwest of town. At 250m wide and 30m high, Dray Nur is the more impressive of the two.

Coffee lovers will want to visit the **World of Coffee Museum**, housed in a stunningly modern interpretation of an ethnic longhouse. Inside, there are more than 10,000 coffee-related artefacts showcasing the history, production and enjoyment of coffee in Vietnam and abroad. Some of the coffee farms around Buon Ma Thuot also offer tours that take visitors from berry to brew, like **Aeroco Coffee** or **Coffee Farm Experience**; the latter is a recent collaboration between Nestlé and the Western Highlands Agriculture & Forestry Science Institute.

Where Nature & Culture Meet

Buon Ma Thuot is all about the outdoors, including swimming underneath the waterfalls and hiking in the national parks to see how the vegetation changes with altitude. Trek up the 1445m-high Chu Yang Lak in **Chu Yang Sin National Park** (p174) for phenomenal views, with bonus interactions with the M'nong and Ede minority groups.

Also try *ruou can*, a strong rice wine mixed with herbs collected in the mountains by the Ede people. There are rituals associated with drinking this wine, fermented in large earthen jugs, which makes imbibing all the more memorable.

■ Recommended by Dinh Hoang, *tour guide with* To Ong Adventure @toong_trips

33 Wellness **ESCAPES**

VEGETARIAN | TRADITIONAL MEDICINE | MUD BATHS

████ While Vietnam doesn't immediately spring to mind as a wellness destination like some of its neighbours, there are certainly many experiences to be had by the health-conscious traveller, ranging from a relaxing massage by blind therapists to full-on cupping, coining and acupuncture sessions.

TAN DAO DUY/GETTY IMAGES ©

🗺 **How to**

Finding vegetarian options Look for the word *chay* (vegetarian) appended to the name of a dish, for example *pho chay* (vegetarian noodle soup). While there are vegetarian eateries everywhere, they are most commonly found near pagodas and temples.

Tipping While tipping isn't common in Vietnam, the one exception is massages. Most rates are for the massage only; patrons are expected to tip almost as much to the therapist. A minimum of 100,000d for an hour's massage is the norm. If in doubt, check with reception.

TRAN QUI THINH/SHUTTERSTOCK ©

Far left Yoga, Ho Chi Minh City
Bottom left Museum of Traditional
Vietnamese Medicine **Near left** Mud
bath, Nha Trang

THE HIGHLANDS EXPERIENCES

Vietnam's Best Wellness Experiences

Museum of Traditional Vietnamese Medicine (Ho Chi Minh City)
Everything you need to know about traditional Vietnamese medicine under one roof.

Dao Spa Sapanapro (Sapa) An exhilarating herbal bath of the Red Dao people known to treat arthritis and skin conditions.

National Hospital of Acupuncture (Hanoi)
The real deal if you're seeking a traditional, non-invasive therapy or have always wanted to try acupuncture.

Cat Tuong Quan (Hue)
Immerse yourself in Zen with a day of meditation, yoga and a vegetarian cooking class within this tranquil garden complex.

I-Resort Hot Mineral Springs (Nha Trang) A modern facility with mud baths, hot-spring pools and waterfalls makes for a fun wellness outing.

■ Recommended by **Thuy Do,** *founder of Wellness Vietnam* @WellnessVietnam

Eat your veggies Vietnamese food features lots of vegetables and fresh herbs, with meat viewed more as a condiment than the main ingredient. Buddhists and members of Vietnam's home-grown religion of Caodaism also practise vegetarianism, at least on the first and 15th (new and full moon) of each lunar month, when eateries put on extra plant-based options.

'Evil wind' The Vietnamese often attribute sudden illness to an 'evil wind' and seek to relieve it using a coin *(cao gio)* to firmly scrape the skin to bring the toxic elements out, usually with the addition of medicated oil. Cupping *(giac hoi)* uses small glass cups, partially vacuumed (by a pump or a flaming cotton-topped baton) and set on the skin to draw out the pain and increase circulation. Cupping is painless, while coining involves moderate skin irritation – still, people with a cold swear by it.

Parklife Because homes are typically small, the Vietnamese love being outdoors. At the local park, you'll find free exercise machines, people playing badminton or kicking around a shuttlecock, and even join-in group calisthenics. Pay the nominal fee to the instructor and join the fray of people doing choreographed dance moves accompanied by a boom box.

Get muddy Bathing in mud and mineral water is an age-old treatment said to improve circulation, rejuvenate the skin and help with pain relief. Nha Trang is known for its many mud-bath centres; Hue and Vung Tau have natural hot springs. In the north around Sapa, the Red Dao people are known for medicinal baths using mountain herbs.

Listings

Heritage Highlights

KoTam Ecotourism Destination

Just 9km from Buon Ma Thuot, this attraction is dedicated to preserving and promoting the culture of the central highlands with guided tours of longhouses, authentic meals, and festivals throughout the year, all in gorgeous natural surrounds of forests and flower fields.

Cu Lan Village

This 30-hectare destination modelled after a K'Ho village is about 45 minutes northwest of Dalat at the foot of Lang Bian Mountain. Activities include touring the village to learn more about Dalat's ethnic groups, walks and 4WD tours in the surrounding forests, and more.

Bao Dai's Palace

Not to be confused with Bao Dai's villa by Lak Lake, this home of Vietnam's last emperor features a mix of modern and indigenous architectural elements right in Buon Ma Thuot. The decor is mid-20th century along with some cultural artefacts on display.

Coffee 101

Horizon Coffee $

Perched on a hill just 10 minutes from Dalat's city centre, Horizon Coffee is all about the views over the surrounding pine forests. The cutesy decor makes for perfect selfies.

Cafe Tui Mo To $

About 15 minutes east of Dalat towards Trai Mat, Cafe Tui Mo To boasts gorgeous views over the surrounding greenhouses and valleys, the perfect place for a cuppa in its garden of white chrysanthemums.

Me Linh Coffee Garden $

It's worth the 30-minute drive into the countryside west of Dalat for a great cup of coffee and tranquil 360-degree views over coffee plants and a lake backed by forested hills.

Trung Nguyen Coffee Village $

Learn about how Buon Ma Thuot coffee is grown and processed at this mini-museum with more than 500 artefacts, then sip a fresh cup of Trung Nguyen coffee in the pretty garden area.

The Great Outdoors

To Ong Adventure

Specialising in adventure and nature travel, To Ong Adventure has tours all across Vietnam, including in Buon Ma Thuot, combining camping, trekking, climbing, kayaking and more.

Chu Yang Sin National Park

Located 60km southeast of Buon Ma Thuot, this 590-sq-km national park boasts steep slopes and narrow valleys centred around the 2442m-high Chu Yang Sin Mountain. Over 20 different ethnic minorities reside in the buffer zone.

Cu Lan Village

Lieng Rowoa Camp

Just by Elephant Falls, about a 50-minute drive from Dalat, Lieng Rowoa has camping sites and a dorm with a BBQ area, kitchen and cosy common room, all surrounded by nature.

Phat Tire Ventures

Canyoning, mountain biking, cycling, rafting, zip lining, hiking – Phat Tire Ventures does it all in Dalat. The company is especially known for its excellent safety record.

Pink Grass Hill

One of Dalat's most sought-after backdrops is its fields of pink grass (particularly in November and December). While there are several sites around town, the best-known location is by Suoi Vang. Come early when there's dew on the ground, making the fields glisten like snow.

Lak Lake

About an hour and a half south of Buon Ma Thuot lies Lak Lake, the largest natural freshwater lake in the central highlands. Rent a boat to explore the lake or visit the fascinating M'nong villages on its shores.

🖊 Regional Cuisine

Banh Trang Nuong Be Lun $

This small eatery in Dalat takes grilled rice paper (both crispy like a pizza or soft like a burrito) to the next level with a tonne of topping choices like egg, dried pork floss, minced pork or beef jerky, all washed down with a glass of milk tea.

Quan Thu $

Grab a low plastic stool and try *bun do,* a Buon Ma Thuot speciality of thick rice noodles in a hearty red broth flavoured with pork bones, crab meat and tomatoes. There's some covered seating, but this is true street food.

Lak Lake

Banh Cuon Thit Nuong Tran Nhat Duat $

Grilled pork wrapped in a sheet of steamed rice flour and served with shredded mango and fresh herbs is a Buon Ma Thuot favourite, especially for breakfast.

Ruou Can Y Mien $$

Y Mien is famous for its traditional Ede-style rice wine aged for at least six months underground. The 1L version in a decorative earthen elephant jug makes for a great gift at this Buon Ma Thuot store.

📷 Instagrammable Spots

Hiep Khach Lau

Fans of Chinese historical movies will want to make a beeline to this whimsical spot in Dalat where you can rent a costume and pose in front of smoking wells, a water wheel and wooden teahouses surrounded by thick bamboo forests.

Hoa Son Dien Trang

Just 20 minutes from the centre of Dalat, Hoa Son Dien Trang is all about natural backdrops, including a swing over the forest, flower fields and platforms that perfectly frame your shot.

Scan to find more things to do in the Highlands online

HO CHI MINH CITY

STREET FOOD | HISTORY | CITY LIFE

Experience
Ho Chi Minh
City online

HO CHI MINH CITY
Trip Builder

Vibrant, friendly and packed with things to do, Ho Chi Minh City (sometimes also called 'Saigon') is Vietnam's largest city and the gateway to the Mekong Delta. Innovative cuisine, a world-class street-food scene and fascinating history all await.

Go on an eating spree along one of the city's famed **food streets** (p204)
🚎 *15min from central HCMC*

 Saigon

Go on a walking tour of Ho Chi Minh City's French-era **heritage buildings** (p182)
City centre

DISTRICT 10

Sample Vietnam-inspired craft beer at **BiaCraft Artisan Ales** (p208)
🚎 *10min from central HCMC*

Explore Vietnam's largest **Chinatown**, ending with a dim sum feast (p200)
🚎 *20min from central HCMC*

Learn about Vietnam's modern history through art at the **Museum of Fine Arts** (p189)
🚶 *13min from central HCMC*

Chinatown (2km)

PHU NHUAN
DISTRICT

Thi Nghe Channel

BINH THANH
DISTRICT

Take the kids to a wildly
weird Buddhist **theme park**
(p187)
🚐 35min from central HCMC

Suoi Tien Theme
Park (14km)

Botanic
Gardens

DISTRICT 3

Catch a Vietnamese-themed
acrobatics show at the
Opera House (p187)
City centre

DISTRICT 2

Saigon River

Cong Vien
Van Hoa
Park

DISTRICT 1

Take a
budget-friendly
waterbus ride on the
Saigon River (p196)
🚶 8min from central
HCMC

PHAM
NGU LAO

Have a molecular sphere of
pho at **Anan Saigon** (p192)
🚶 9min from central HCMC

Explore book-
able experiences
in Ho Chi Minh
City

Ben Nghe Channel

1 km
0.5 miles

Practicalities

TAN SON NHAT INTERNATIONAL TERMINAL

TRAN NGOC DUNG/SHUTTERSTOCK ©

ARRIVING

Tan Son Nhat International Airport Located 7km northwest of downtown. Bus 109 (40,000d) departs from both domestic and international terminals and ends at the 23 September Park, near the 'backpacker area'. There's also a taxi rank outside (assigned at random, but you can approach the reliable Mai Linh or Vinasun agents to request a cab ride). You can also order a Grab car, but language difficulties may make meeting up a challenge.

WHEN TO GO

DEC–FEB
Coolest time of the year, with no rain.

MAR–MAY
Occasional rain, with rising temperatures and humidity.

JUN–AUG
Some rain, although light and usually over quickly.

SEP–NOV
Rainy season; heavy downpours typically in the afternoon.

HOW MUCH FOR A

banh mi sandwich
15,000d

taxi to the airport
170,000d

pho noodle soup
35,000d

GETTING AROUND

Cyclos and walking Pedal-powered *cyclos* are a fun way to get around, especially in downtown District 1, but make sure both you and the driver are clear on the route and price before getting on. Walking short distances is an option, but be careful crossing busy streets. Just keep walking at a consistent pace and drivers will drive around you.

Ride sharing Offering both cars and motorbikes, ride-sharing apps are common, especially Grab and Gojek. Sometimes drivers will phone to check that you've actually ordered a ride. Link your credit card for extra convenience.

Taxis Cheap and plentiful, Mai Linh and Vinasun are the most reliable. Both have apps.

EATING & DRINKING

One of the world's best food cities, Ho Chi Minh City draws people and regional specialities from all across Vietnam. From humble street stalls to posh restaurants helmed by Michelin-starred chefs, there's a superb range of dining options. *Pho* and *com tam* (grilled pork over broken rice; pictured top right) are ubiquitous, as are roadside coffee stands (some with high-end coffee machines). The Bui Vien area is good for cheap international eats and late-night beers, but you're never more than a few steps from a cheap, filling meal.

Best craft beer	Must-try contemporary Vietnamese
BiaCraft (p209)	Anan Saigon (p192)

CONNECT & FIND YOUR WAY

Wi-fi Most indoor restaurants and cafes have free wi-fi. Otherwise, a monthly 3G/4G plan is relatively cheap (around 100,000d). Ask the person selling you a Vietnamese SIM to help register.

Navigation Google Maps is your friend. Note that some streets exist in multiple districts – when typing the address, include the district and ward for best results.

MONEY

You can live like a king or a pauper. Booking tours will quickly burn through your budget, but street food and transport within the city are cheap. Cash is king, so pack your wallet with small bills.

WHERE TO STAY

Ho Chi Minh City has a wide range of accommodation options, from super-cheap fan-cooled dorm rooms to glitzy internationally recognised brands.

Neighbourhood	Pro/Con
District 1	Around ĐL Nguyen Hue, Dong Khoi and ĐL Le Loi, you'll be able to walk to the main attractions, but room rates will be higher.
Bui Vien and Pham Ngu Lao	The 'backpacker area' has lots of budget options where younger travellers tend to party. Expect some street noise.
District 3	Quiet and leafy, with a high concentration of historic buildings, You'll need short taxi rides for most places.
Districts 2 and 7	Slightly out of the city centre, but with lots of international restaurants.
Chinatown	A range of budget to midrange hotels. Great food option, but a bit far from the centre.

ON GUARD

Crime is rarely violent, but bag and phone snatching is not unheard of. Be careful with using your phone in public (even on the pavement).

34 A Walk Through
HISTORY

HISTORY | ARCHITECTURE | CULTURE

This easy 1km walk in the heart of downtown Ho Chi Minh City is packed with beautiful buildings dating back more than a century. In between checking out the heritage sites, stop for some retail therapy, an icy craft beer and perhaps even a concert.

🗺️ Trip Notes

What you'll need Bring along a hat, sunscreen and a bottle of water to beat the Saigon heat. While the route takes only 12 minutes to walk from end to end, there are lots of air-conditioned shops along the way to cool off.

Explore more The interiors of these buildings are also worth seeing. Grab a cold beer and enjoy the views from the Caravelle's 9th-floor Saigon Saigon Bar, catch an acrobatic AO Show at the Opera House, or people-watch from one of the trendy cafes at 42 ĐL Nguyen Hue (p210).

📖 Interact with Saigon's History

From the Notre Dame Cathedral, look a few blocks southeast to spot the rooftop from Hugh Van Es' iconic 1975 war photo.

Visit the Hotel Continental (pictured), a favourite spot of writer Graham Greene and Vietnam's famous Communist agent Pham Xuan An.

■ Recommended by **Dang Duong**,
co-founder of Old Compass Travel & Cafe @oldcompass travelvietnam

02 Just across the street, the working **Central Post Office** dates back to 1891. Look for the oversized vintage maps and the railway-station-like design with plaques honouring scientists and inventors.

03 Completed in 1897, the **Opera House** was inspired by Paris' Petit Palais. To see the plush 468-seat oval auditorium, book a reasonably priced ticket for a concert or ballet.

04 Opened in 1959, the **Caravelle Hotel** was 'the' spot for foreign journalists covering the American War. It's said that they could even watch air strikes from the rooftop terrace.

01 Modelled after the one in Paris, Saigon's **Notre Dame Cathedral** was inaugurated in 1880. Inside, notice the beautiful glass windows and a shrine dedicated to Vietnamese martyrs.

05 Imagine **ĐL Nguyen Hue** as the canal it once was linking the Saigon River to the city. Vehicle-free at night, the boulevard comes alive with vendors and street performers.

Cong Vien Van Hoa Park

DL Le Duan

Đ Nguyen Du

ĐL Hai Ba Trung

Đ Dong Khoi

Đ Ly Tu Trong

Đ Le Thanh Ton

Lam Son Square

Đ Nguyen Thiep

Đ Dong Khoi

ĐL Le Loi

DISTRICT 1

ĐL Nguyen Hue

Đ Ham Nghi

Saigon River

0 — 200 m
0 — 0.1 miles

Iconic
SAIGON SIGHTS

01 Bitexco Financial Tower

The city's second-highest building, shaped like a lotus bud, has a 49th-floor helipad and Skydeck.

02 Landmark 81

Vietnam's tallest building has a retail mall at its base, and gorgeous views from the restaurants and cafes at the top.

03 Central Post Office

Graced with vintage tiled floors and an airy train-station-like interior, this working post office dates back to 1891.

04 Reunification Palace

The former seat of South Vietnam's government, this 1960s building has a basement telecommunications centre.

05 Ben Thanh Market

HCMC's most famous market has over 1500 stalls selling everything from fresh produce to kitschy souvenirs.

06 People's Committee Building

The colonial-era facade of HCMC's old Hôtel de Ville is especially pretty when lit up at night.

07 Notre Dame Cathedral

Built in the late 1800s, this red-brick neo-Romanesque church boasts 60m-high bell towers.

08 Opera House

This stunning building from 1897 hosts ballets, concerts, musicals and more.

09 Bui Vien

In the heart of the 'backpacker district', Đ Bui Vien is the place to mingle with fellow travellers over cheap beer and good eats.

10 Thien Hau Pagoda

Giant coils of smoky incense give this 19th-century temple an aura of mystery.

11 Phu My Bridge

View the skyline from Vietnam's first cable-stayed bridge.

12 Tan Dinh Church

This raucously pink church features a six-bell octagonal tower and Italian marble altars.

13 Turtle Lake

This roundabout with its many food vendors is a favourite hang-out spot.

35 WITH KIDS
in Tow

FAMILY-FRIENDLY | PERFORMANCE ART | AMUSEMENT PARKS

████ While Ho Chi Minh City has lots of international family-friendly activities like bowling, movie theatres and malls, it seems a bit of a waste to do something you could well do at home. Instead, opt for activities with a bit of local culture, ranging from water puppetry and bamboo acrobatics to Buddhist theme parks and double-decker touring.

POS2TOS/SHUTTERSTOCK ©

🗺 How to

Getting around Ho Chi Minh City isn't very pedestrian-friendly, especially for small kids. Just crossing the street seems daunting, not to mention motorbikes driving on the pavement. Take a taxi when possible or opt for a vintage *cyclo* in the city centre.

Toddler alert Vietnamese tend to gush over babies and toddlers, so prepare the little ones for the occasional pat or poke from a well-meaning local.

Travel light Actual sidewalks can be few and far between. Parents can opt for a carrier instead of a bulky stroller to navigate the streets.

SOLARISYS/SHUTTERSTOCK ©

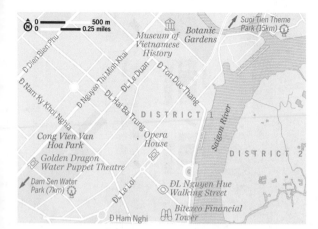

Top left Golden Dragon Water Puppet Theatre **Bottom left** Dam Sen Water Park

Kid-Friendly Dishes

Pho Ask for a *to em be* (baby bowl) of Vietnam's ubiquitous noodle-soup dish, a smaller portion served without onion, herbs and pepper.

Xiu mai Soft, succulent pork meatballs cooked in tomato sauce can be eaten with rice or inside a *banh mi* (baguette).

Bun cha Our kids eat this Hanoi speciality by combining the seasoned pork patties with the rice noodles, ignoring the slices of pork belly, lettuce and herbs served alongside.

Hoanh thanh A Chinese adaptation, the Vietnamese wonton is filled with pork and prawn. *Mi hoanh thanh* (with egg noodles) is probably the most child-pleasing version.

Che ba mau A tasty version of this cold, sugary snack has a custardy yellow layer of mung beans, green strips of pandan jelly and red kidney beans, floating in sweetened coconut cream.

■ Recommended by Barbara Adam & Vu Vo, *founders of Saigon Street Eats @therealsaigonstreeteats*

HO CHI MINH CITY EXPERIENCES

Puppet theatre Originating as storytelling in the Red River Delta, water puppetry entertains both young and old. At the **Golden Dragon Water Puppet Theatre**, colourful wooden puppets (controlled by puppeteers hidden behind a bamboo screen) on the watery stage are accompanied by live traditional music. While there's Vietnamese narration for scenes re-enacting folk tales or legends, it's easy enough to follow the action.

Water world Adults might raise an eyebrow at the Buddhist-themed attractions at the 105-hectare **Suoi Tien Theme Park** with its statues of dragons, unicorns, tortoises and phoenixes, but kids will see it as a massive playground complete with a water park, roller coaster, snow castle and mini-zoo. To beat the heat closer to town, the 50-hectare **Dam Sen Water Park** has a wave pool, slides, a zip line and other attractions.

Hop on, hop off With its heat and humidity, hardly anyone walks around HCMC except for tourists. Instead, opt for the double-decker hop-on/hop-off bus which covers 10 stops in District 1, including family-friendly attractions like the **Museum of Vietnamese History**, the 68-storey **Bitexco Financial Tower** (with a mall and observation Skydeck) and **ĐL Nguyen Hue** walking street.

Dance for me A troupe of hip-hop dancers, parkour athletes and circus performers present the high-energy **AO Show** – part acrobatics, part storytelling, and thoroughly fun. Props include traditional Vietnamese bamboo items typical of the countryside. Parents will enjoy gazing at the ornate interior of the 1897 **Opera House**.

36 Art
EDUCATION

ART | MUSEUMS | ARCHITECTURE

You don't have to be an art aficionado to appreciate these opportunities to learn about Vietnam's history and culture through art. Gain insight into where Vietnam has been, through ancient artefacts from other civilisations – as well as where it's heading, through contemporary works.

🗺 How to

When to go Many of Vietnam's businesses and government-operated facilities close during lunchtime and some aren't open every day, so check the schedule before you go. These are also good spots to escape the heat, so plan on arriving in late morning or early afternoon when it's hottest outside.

What to buy Consider supporting these museums, galleries and studios by purchasing a unique souvenir for an art lover back home, or enhance your experience with a hands-on workshop offered by some of the independent galleries.

Museum of Vietnamese History

Next to the Botanical Gardens, this beautifully housed museum presents Vietnamese history through more than 10,000 artefacts arranged chronologically. In particular, the Buddhist- and Hindu-influenced sculptures from the Funan (1st to 6th centuries) and the Champa (2nd to 17th centuries) civilisations are outstanding, as are the brocades and copper urns from the Nguyen dynasty (1802–1945).

Museum of Fine Arts

While the museum also displays ancient art, its 20th-century collection is where it shines, featuring notable Vietnamese masters like Nguyen Gia Tri, whose oversized lacquer paintings fuse Western aesthetics with traditional Vietnamese techniques. Also check out the fascinating war-inspired art depicting strong, smiling soldiers and admire the art-deco building itself.

🛍 Art Replicas

In addition to painting Vietnam-themed works, many university-trained artists supplement their own art with reproductions of famous paintings done in the same style as the original. If you dream of hanging a Van Gogh or a Klimt, settle for the next best thing from the shops along **Đ Bui Vien** and **ĐL Nguyen Hue**.

Top left Museum of Fine Arts **Bottom left** Museum of Vietnamese History **Top right** Bodhisattva Lokesvara statue, Museum of Vietnamese History

Salon Saigon

Set in a spacious historical mansion, Salon Saigon showcases contemporary artists expressing Vietnam's culture and history through reinterpreted traditional mediums. It also hosts screenings, artist talks and other programs. Order a cup of tea and a snack and browse the fine trilingual library of Vietnamese and Asian culture and contemporary creation.

Street Style

Originally from London, woodcut printmaker and illustrator Jack Clayton draws inspiration from typical Vietnamese phrases and Saigon's urban environment, including an entire series based on street scenes from the little-touristed District 4. His woodcuts are often made from just one piece of wood, incorporating the natural lines of the wood into the image. His beautifully detailed hand-drawn illustrations highlight unique aspects of Vietnam's

Vietnam's Contemporary Art

Over the past two decades, Vietnamese contemporary artists have become increasingly integrated into the mainstream of international art practices. Once confined to traditional motifs and mediums, Vietnamese contemporary art now embraces all forms of modern practice, from painting to installation, video and performance art. Mid-career artists like Pham Huy Thong have widened the focus of their work to address the society around them and give their perspectives on the tremendous changes since the country's reopening. Perhaps most exciting is the rise of a young generation of painters – still the country's strength – like Pham Thanh Toan, whose work would look modern hanging anywhere.

■ **Insights from Craig Thomas,** *founder of the Craig Thomas Gallery* @craigthomasgallery

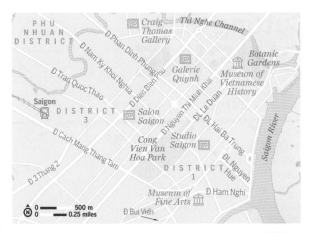

Left *Family, Enid, circa 1982* by Trong Gia Nguyen, Galerie Quynh **Below** *Waiting for Jobs* by Nguyen Hung Son, Craig Thomas Gallery

history and culture. Browse the whimsical prints on the ground floor of his District 4 **workshop**, then head upstairs to make your own woodcut.

With a degree in Egyptian archaeology, sketch artist Richie Fawcett can often be found on a balcony or under a tree documenting Saigon's fast-disappearing heritage buildings. See his in-credibly detailed pen and ink drawings of the city's ever-changing skyline at **The Studio Saigon**. He might even invite you into the speakeasy hidden behind the studio for one of his signature cocktails inspired by Saigon's colourful neighbourhoods.

Contemporary Art

Opened in 2009 by its namesake artist and curator, **Craig Thomas Gallery** showcases work by two dozen emerging and mid-career contemporary artists from Hanoi, Saigon and Hue, some of whom are exhibiting commercially for the first time. Works include paintings, sculptures and mixed media.

Established in 2003, **Galerie Quynh** has emerged as the city's preeminent contemporary art gallery. Its sometimes controversial, often thought-provoking exhibitions bring modern life and social issues to the fore and aim to elevate the visual literacy of the Vietnamese public. Check the gallery's Facebook page for talks, lectures, publications and collaborations.

37 Cutting-Edge
CUISINE

CONTEMPORARY CUISINE | CRAFT COCKTAILS | CHOCOLATE

More than a melting pot of regional dishes, Ho Chi Minh City leads the modernisation of Vietnamese cuisine, elevating it with better ingredients and innovative cooking techniques, and reimagining familiar flavours. At the creative forefront are chefs returning to Vietnam from abroad, marrying their international experience with traditional Vietnamese cuisine.

🗺 **How to**

Cost Expect to pay significantly more for these innovative food and drink experiences, ranging from 285,000d for a souped-up *pho* with foie gras and truffle at Anan Saigon to 1,599,000d for a six-course tasting menu at Nous Dine.

Plan ahead Peruse the menu before you go and try the street-food (or regular) version of the dishes you intend to order. You'll then better appreciate how these restaurants have creatively reinvented the dish while retaining its basic components.

Map details:
0 — 500 m
0 — 0.25 miles

Botanic Gardens
Đ Đinh Tien Hoang
Đ Điện Biên Phủ
Blanc Restaurant Saigon
Đ Nguyễn Thị Minh Khai
ĐL Hai Ba Trung
ĐL Le Duan
Đ Nam Ky Khoi Nghia
Đ Lý Tự Trọng
Nous Dine
Cong Vien Van Hoa Park
DISTRICT 1
ĐL Nguyen Hue
Summer Experiment
ĐL Le Loi
Anan Saigon
Đ Ham Nghi
PHAM NGU LAO
ĐL Tran Hung Dao
Maison Marou
Đ Ban Chuong

Anan Saigon One of the city's contemporary cuisine pioneers, Anan is known for Vietnamese food with a modern twist. Grab a *banh xeo* taco or a roast-duck Dalat pizza on the ground floor, a Vietnamese coffee martini at **Nhau Nhau bar** (2nd floor), a molecular sphere of *pho* at **Pot au Pho** (3rd floor), or a 'phojito' on the rooftop bar with views of the city skyline.

Nous Dine Vietnam's first capsule restaurant feels like an episode of *Top Chef Vietnam*, where only eight guests get to sit up close to the pass and enjoy the food theatre, from cooking to plating to eating. Seasonal tasting menus focus on

Top right Blanc Restaurant & Noir Restaurant (p211) **Bottom right** Slow-cooked short ribs (*Galbi-jjim*), Nous Dine

JAMES PHAM/LONELY PLANET ©

THAO BUI ©

⚗ Summer Experiment

Build your own gin- or vodka-based cocktail with a mixer and botanical concoctions at Summer Experiment, the only Saigon establishment to be named on Asia's Best Bars 2021 list.

quality local ingredients, modern techniques and flawless presentation to deliver familiar flavours with flair, like the lotus-seed ice cream with longan shaved ice.

Maison Marou A cafe, shop and mini-factory, Maison Marou is a chocoholic's dream. There's a cacao-bean roaster on site, and a small workshop where the beans are turned into all manner of chocolate delights, like the limited-edition chocolate bar inspired by *pho* spices. The single-origin hot chocolate with cinnamon and chilli is a dream.

Blanc Restaurant Saigon Set in a remodelled heritage home, Blanc is a sophisticated dining experience both in decor and eclectic menu. Expect elevated versions of Vietnamese classics, like the *pho* consommé with caramelised onions and Wagyu-beef brisket, or the fresh Vietnamese fig salad with Brie and roasted pine nuts. Most of the service staff are hearing-impaired; use the guide to communicate in sign language.

LUCHEZAR/GETTY IMAGES ©

Contemporary Gastronomy

GIVING VIETNAMESE FOOD A MODERN MAKEOVER

Vietnamese food abroad has hit the mainstream, with *pho* and *banh mi* joints everywhere there's Vietnamese diaspora. Back in Saigon, traditional flavours are getting an exciting makeover thanks to returning chefs and a look inwards for inspiration.

Vietnamese cuisine has had a long evolution, incorporating influences from China and France and, more recently, imported ingredients resulting in dishes like *pho* noodle soup with Wagyu beef, Iberico-pork spring rolls or an over-the-top US$100 *banh mi* featuring foie gras and truffle mayonnaise. 'Every dish will be better with better ingredients,' says Hoang Tung, co-founder and head chef of Å by TUNG. 'The older generation did not have the opportunity to use quality products, but if we can make great food with regular products, imagine what we can do with premium ingredients.'

However, chefs are increasingly looking inwards to take Vietnamese cuisine to the next level, experimenting with and showcasing local ingredients. 'There is a lot of pride in using locally sourced ingredients in an innovative way, without overcomplicating recipes so that the real flavours of the ingredients really shine through,' says Mai The Anh of Lady Trieu Gin, the craft spirits company behind an experimental range of gins called The Lab Series. Its latest creations draw inspiration from Vietnam's incredible regional biodiversity, employing botanicals like star anise and wild forest pepper in its Mekong Delta Dry Gin, or cardamom, cassia and pomelo in its Hoi An Spice Road Gin.

Vietnamese ingredients are even appearing in desserts and cocktails, once squarely Western territory. 'When I first arrived in Vietnam, there was a cultural vacuum in terms of cocktails,' says mixologist Richie Fawcett. 'But more recently, young Vietnamese bartenders are finding hyper-regional, hard-to-find botanicals and ingredients sitting right under their noses, like magnolia berries and cubeb pepper from Kon Tum which are a step up from lemongrass and basil.'

Left *Pho* with Wagyu beef **Middle** Esta Eatery **Right** Maison Marou Chocolate

'The dessert front is even more radical,' says chef Peter Franklin of Vietnam's dessert scene, which typically tends to be simply fresh fruit or sometimes *che,* a cooked soup-like treat with unconventional ingredients like beans, corn and potatoes. Chef Peter's latest foray into innovating sweet treats is his *nuoc mam* ice cream. 'It's like salted caramel, but instead of salt, I'm using fish sauce for more umami flavour,' he explains. He's also collaborating with the wildly popular Marou Chocolate brand to create bonbons that combine fish sauce with single-origin chocolate.

> *'Nuoc mam* ice cream is like salted caramel, but instead of salt, I'm using fish sauce.'

What's unique about this latest trend is how it's sweeping through the entire gastronomic scene. 'It's not only chefs, but winemakers, bartenders and other culinary artists who are seeking to infuse Vietnamese flavours into their products,' says Francis Thuan Tran, co-founder and executive chef of Esta Eatery, where ingredients like Buddha's hand (a citrusy fruit) and wild beans and leaves complement Hmong-style grilled pork jowl.

Francis is part of the wave of innovators who are letting their experiences abroad – living, working, and travelling – inspire their cooking and each other to push the creative limits of contemporary Vietnamese food. Whatever the direction, though, one truth remains: 'You can change the ingredients and the techniques as long as you still deliver Vietnamese flavours,' says Peter. 'Flavour defines the cuisine and the culture.'

✖ Innovative Eats

Esta Eatery is doing something special in Saigon. They don't shy away from taking risks in the kitchen, and it shows in spades in their amazing rotating menus.

If you're looking to experience amazing cocktails that delicately balance simplicity and creativity using local ingredients and inspiration, go no further than **The Studio Saigon** by the mad chemist and brilliant artist Richie Fawcett, who actually pioneered the movement behind creative cocktails in Saigon.

I love what the team at **Bom Gastronomy** is doing, taking bold risks to transform and even elevate Vietnamese cuisine without being pretentious. They have a genuine desire to create a narrative around the beauty in Vietnam's rich culinary history.

■ Recommended by **Daniel Nguyen,** *owner of Nous Dine.* @dan.nugu

38
A River Runs
THROUGH IT

WATER SPORTS | CRUISING | CYCLING

■■■■ While casual visitors to Ho Chi Minh City may only catch glimpses of the Saigon River along the southern end of downtown District 1, activities on or by the river offer a surprisingly relaxing take on this otherwise chaotic city. From water sports to a leisurely riverside brunch, take to the water for a completely different perspective.

🗺️ How to

Riverside walk The small park-like Bach Dang Jetty (from where the waterbus leaves) is the closest thing to a public boardwalk where visitors can take a short, leisurely stroll along the river.

Bridges of HCMC For another vantage point, consider walking over one of the city's bridges. The pedestrian-only Anh Sao Bridge in District 7 spans the Thay Tieu Canal and is especially beautiful when lit up at night.

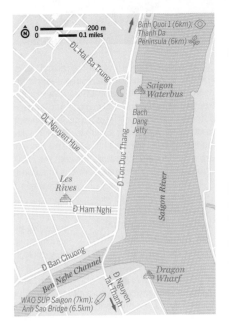

Cruising Explore river life with a host of cruise options. Dinner cruises leave from **Dragon Wharf**, the original commercial port of Saigon, and make for a fun evening with live music and impressive views of the glittering skyline. To see more of the city, try a sunset speedboat cruise with

Les Rives (p210). For something more budget-friendly, the **Saigon Waterbus** travels from downtown Bach Dang Jetty up the river to Thu Duc and back. Initially designed as an alternative for commuters, it's become a favourite with tourists out for a leisurely boat ride.

Top right Anh Sao Bridge
Bottom right Binh Quoi 1

PAUL EVAN GREEN/SHUTTERSTOCK ©

🚲 Cycling Thanh Da

Known as the 'green lung of Ho Chi Minh City', Thanh Da peninsula has swaths of rice fields, fishing ponds, coconut trees and little canals best explored by bicycle.

Kitschy country At the very end of Thanh Da peninsula, **Binh Quoi 1** occupies more than 3 hectares designed to look like the Mekong Delta, complete with a water wheel, lotus ponds and giant lily pads (no, they don't support the weight of a human). There's a popular buffet on weekend evenings, but the à la carte restaurant has nice river views during the day.

Stand-up paddleboarding There's no better way to get up close and personal with the Saigon River than by joining one of the many SUP groups that take to the canals right in the city and in the mangroves south in Can Gio. Most clubs offer lessons, rentals and tours. Hawaiian-owned **WAO SUP Saigon** offers lessons in a swimming pool for beginners and even SUP yoga classes. Call a day ahead to check the tides.

TIENDUC1102/SHUTTERSTOCK ©

39
Exploring
DISTRICT 2

ART | RIVER VIEWS | SPORTS

■■■■■ Home to big-spending expats, District 2 with its tree-lined streets, large single homes and international schools can feel more like Anytown, USA, than Vietnam. Sometimes called Thao Dien (after one of its wards), it's an interesting place to visit with a robust eating and drinking scene and great riverside views, especially if you want a quick break from sightseeing.

🗺 How to

Getting there From downtown Ho Chi Minh City, a 15-minute drive across the Saigon Bridge takes you to District 2. Attractions are rather spaced out, so it's best to go by scooter or taxi. Some of the upscale restaurants and hotels also offer speedboat service if you'd like to arrive in style.

Expat bubble Together with District 7, District 2 is where many expats live so it's worth checking out if you're thinking about making a move to HCMC.

HO NGOC BINH/GETTY IMAGES ©

River views One of the best things about District 2 is its views of the Saigon River. **The Deck Saigon** has excellent contemporary pan-Asian fare, while the stylish bar does great cocktails (half-price at sunset). For something more wallet-friendly but with the same views, the **BoatHouse** offers international comfort food with live music most nights. For a splurge, stay at **Mia Saigon**, a luxe boutique hotel where you can laze the day away by the riverside pool. Or enjoy the pool with river views with a day pass at lovely **Villa Song Saigon**.

Above View over Thao Dien ward
Top right Nighttime, District 2
Bottom right The Deck Saigon

🍺 **Dining & Drinks**

District 2 (and Thao Dien ward, in particular) is a great eating and drinking hub, especially along **Đ Xuan Thuy**, **Đ Thao Dien** and **Ngo Quang Huy** streets with their craft-beer joints, trendy cafes and upscale restaurants.

The arts Expats looking to decorate their homes frequent the art galleries here. Even if you aren't looking to buy, **Factory** is a wonderful contemporary arts centre with curated exhibitions, workshops, talks and film screenings. Afterwards, stop in at nearby **MAD House** for one of the best burgers in town. If you want to create art, **VinSpace** art studio has workshops for kids and adults.

The world of sports District 2 is home to fun sports venues, like the rock-climbing wall and skate park at **Saigon Outcast**, which also hosts flea markets, family days and outdoor movie screenings. HCMC's first ice rink is at **Vincom Mega Mall**, where cute plastic animals help newbies keep their balance. Or let off some energy at **Jump Arena**, the biggest trampoline park in Vietnam. There's also a foam pit, climbing wall, airbag for the kids and more.

Time Travel in
CHINATOWN

ARCHITECTURE | FOOD | HISTORY

▬▬▬ Spend a leisurely couple of hours on a walking tour of Vietnam's largest Chinatown to uncover the historic vibe this district exudes, with pagodas smoky with incense, colourful communal halls and one of the best dim sum restaurants in the city.

🗺 Trip Notes

Getting here/around Grab a taxi and make your way to the starting point at Binh Tay Market. The 2.4km-long walking route is rather straightforward, with only a few big streets to cross.

Recommended read For more detailed walking tours of Ho Chi Minh City, including central and west Cholon, pick up the excellent *Exploring Saigon-Cho Lon: Vanishing Heritage of Ho Chi Minh City* by Tim Doling, available at the larger Fahasa bookshops.

🛒 A Tale of Two Cities

Founded in 1778 by Chinese emigrants, Chinatown (also known as Cholon, literally 'large market') was originally a city on its own, separated by 11km of swampland from then Saigon. The French made Saigon the political and administrative capital of Cochinchina, while Cholon was its economic capital.

0 | 500 m
0 | 0.25 miles

Ⓝ

D 3 Thang 2

DISTRICT 10

ĐL Nguyen Chi Thanh

DISTRICT 5

04 For a peek into an ethnic Chinese neighbourhood, head to the alley known as **Hao Sy Phuong**. The colourful houses make for great photo backdrops; be discreet as the homes are close together.

01 Start by wandering the stalls of **Binh Tay Market**, rebuilt in the 1920s. The Chinese architectural elements include the two dragons above its clock tower and more guarding the courtyard.

Đ Hong Bang

Đ Chau Van Liem

Đ Luong Nhu Hoc

Đ Trieu Quang Phuc

Đ Tan Da

Đ Ngo Quyen

ĐL Tran Hung Dao

ĐL Tran Hung Dao

ĐL Thap Muoi

Đ Go Cong

ĐL Hai Thuong Lan Ong

Đ Phung Hung

Đ B Phan Van Khoe

Đ Chu Van An

Đ Ngo Nhan Tinh

Tau Hu Channel

05 End up at **Cat Tuong**, a favourite for authentic dim sum and other dishes. At lunchtime there are often eclectic performances of Chinese opera in the open-air dining area.

02 At the **Nghia Nhuan Assembly Hall**, look up at the giant coils of incense suspended from the ceiling and check out the gorgeous textured wall tiles in the rear, a fusion of Chinese, Vietnamese and French influences.

03 One of Cholon's oldest temples, the compact **Nhi Phu Temple** (aka Ong Bon Pagoda) is ornately decorated. Soak in the gorgeous wall panels and the mosaic dragons on the roof.

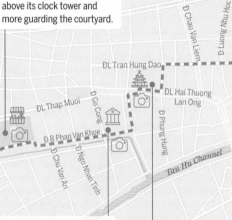

■ By Tim Doling

Tim is the author of historical guide-
books on Saigon-Cholon, Hue and
Quang Nam (historicvietnam.com)

PHOTO CREDIT: MICHAEL ARNOLD

TIM DOLING/LONELY PLANET ©

Saving Saigon

CONSERVATION ADVOCACY MAKES AN IMPACT ONLINE

In the headlong rush for development, hundreds of Saigon's old buildings and streetscapes have fallen victim to the wrecking ball. With no NGOs to lobby for the protection of surviving heritage structures, campaigners have turned to social media to raise awareness and press for change.

Saigon's architecture reflects its multicultural history. Many neighbourhoods were shaped by Vietnamese and Chinese communal houses, assembly halls, temples, pagodas and markets. Then came French colonial architecture in its many forms, subtly adapted to local climatic conditions – on a walk around the city centre, visitors can experience neoclassical, 'Indochinois' fusion, art deco, early modernist and utilitarian structures from the 1880s to the 1940s. In the same period, Indian settlers established temples and mosques. Since the 1950s, Southern Vietnamese modernist architecture has emerged as the dominant style for private residences and shophouses.

The economic growth and urbanisation of recent decades has brought many improvements, but its impact on built heritage has been severe. In a city designated primarily as an economic hub, the preservation of old buildings has never been a government priority. A land-use master plan approved in March 2008 by HCMC People's Committee called for protection of the city's historic core in Districts 1 and 3. However, when high-end development projects east of the river began to stall, this plan was abandoned and authorities began to green-light new office, retail and residential projects in the low-rise city centre.

The absence of legal protection or even of a basic inventory of historic buildings has since permitted the destruction of hundreds of such buildings in the name of modernisation. A 1924 Lafayette-era department store with a priceless Moroccan-mosaic stairway was bulldozed to make way for a 40-storey mall and subway station. A 26-hectare shipyard complex – with late-19th-century French industrial architecture, which many had hoped

Left Catinat Building **Middle** Jamia Al Muslimin Mosque **Right** Art-deco buildings, District 1

would be repurposed as museums, shops and restaurants – was cleared to build luxury apartments. Without guidance or financial support from government, old buildings in private hands have fared particularly badly, although a few have been repurposed to house retail stores and cafes.

Supporters of heritage conservation have turned to social media in an attempt to halt the destruction. In recent years, heritage networking groups like Dai Quan Sat Di San Saigon, Di San Viet and Cho Lon 堤岸 Xua Va Nay, and architecture projects like Tan Man Kien Tru, have proliferated on Facebook, nurturing interest in Saigon's heritage and raising awareness of its ongoing destruction. Crucially, these groups have afforded an unprecedented opportunity to lobby and petition the authorities, urging them to protect surviving built heritage and use it to provide additional leisure opportunities and help attract higher-paying and longer-staying cultural tourists.

> A 1924 Lafayette-era department store with a priceless Moroccan-mosaic stairway was bulldozed to make way for a 40-storey mall and subway station.

The success of a 2018 social-media campaign to preserve the 1882 Government Secretariat building and the People's Committee decision that same year to draw up a preliminary shortlist of protected historic buildings suggest that this tactic has begun to bear fruit. But in the absence of a specialised municipal heritage agency with a budget and a plan, it remains to be seen whether the needs of modernisation and urban renewal can effectively be rebalanced with the conservation of the city's surviving architectural heritage.

🏛 Catinat Building

The art-deco Catinat Building was built in 1926–27 as upmarket offices and apartments by the Société Urbaine Foncière Indochinoise, whose name is still prominently posted on the upper walls. Its most famous tenant was the US Consulate, which suffered a devastating bomb attack on 23 November 1941, reportedly perpetrated by the occupying Japanese military. Two weeks later, Pearl Harbor was attacked and the consulate closed. Today, the five-storey building is home to numerous chic cafes, restaurants and boutiques – take the cage elevator to the top and explore the building floor by floor.

41

Saigon's Best Food
STREETS

EATING | STREET FOOD | CITY LIFE

▬▬▬ While it seems you can't go 10 steps without seeing something to eat, there are a few streets that have built up a reputation for being a foodie's paradise. Some cater to students while others specialise in a certain type of food. What it means for the diner, though, is a whole range of delicious bites all within steps of each other.

BRUCE YUANYUE BI/GETTY IMAGES ©

🗺 **How to**

When to go There's never really a bad time to go on an eating spree. Note that some dishes, like noodle soups and broken rice, are mainly served in the mornings, while other streets come to life at night.

How to order Don't expect English menus

outside the most tourist-ed areas. However, two phrases are imperative: *dac biet* ('special', pronounced 'duhk bee-uht') and *day du* ('everything', pronounced 'daay doo'). They both mean the same: 'give me the best version of this dish'.

PETE BURANA/SHUTTERSTOCK ©

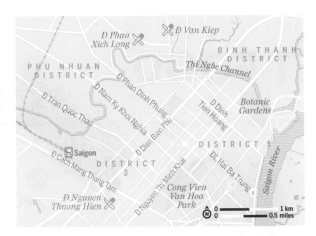

Top left *Banh mi* stand **Bottom left** Sweet corn vendor

Đ Nguyen Thuong Hien, District 3 Along Đ Nguyen Thuong Hien from the Cach Mang Thang 8 roundabout to Đ Nguyen Thi Minh Khai, you'll find a dozen or so little seafood restaurants. Order off the menu, or pick your live seafood at market prices and have it cooked to order. Sautéed with garlic, steamed with coconut milk, grilled and topped with scallion oil – you can have it any way you like it. Most places have indoor seating, or grab a stool at a plastic table outside and wash down your meal with some ice-cold Vietnamese beer.

Đ Van Kiep, Binh Thanh District Practically every home along short but sweet Đ Van Kiep sells food of some sort. You won't find any fancy restaurants here. Instead, it's long-established mom-and-pop eateries that span the gamut of home-cooked dishes at very reasonable prices. Enjoy a steaming plate of wok-fried meat and veggies atop crispy noodles for just 55,000d at number 111 or a selection of steamed dim sum dumplings at number 159. The key is to eat small portions as you go.

Đ Phan Xich Long, Phu Nhuan District You'll be hard-pressed to find a denser concentration of eateries anywhere else in Saigon. From sit-down Chinese to curbside crab soup with bubble-tea stalls and restaurants serving Korean, Japanese, Thai and more thrown in for good measure, the choices are overwhelming. Perhaps start with an ear of grilled corn slathered with scallion oil at number 159, followed by a steaming bowl of noodles topped with roast chicken around the corner at 147 Hoa Lan.

ⓘ **Tips for a First-Time Visitor**

Vietnam has some of the most diverse and delicious street food in the world. As a general rule, it's good to follow the locals and look for the places that have a lot of people, but do also explore small eateries in out-of-the-way places that have only a few customers. When visiting a new city, ask some knowledgeable people to recommend local specialities and to name the places that serve the best version of each dish. This is a good place to start your culinary adventure and learn more about the local culture.

■ Insights from Peter Cuong Franklin, *chef and founder of Anan Saigon @petercuongfranklin*

Must-Try
STREET FOOD

01 Banh xeo
Use a large lettuce leaf to wrap this pork, shrimp and beansprout crêpe like a burrito.

02 Banh canh cua
Thick tapioca noodles in a rich pork broth with chunks of crab makes this an umami bomb.

03 Banh mi
A crispy baguette stuffed with an omelette for breakfast, or with cold cuts and pickles for a cheap, filling meal.

04 Bo kho
A thick stew with chunks of beef and carrots and a hint of cinnamon. Enjoy over noodles or sop it up with a baguette.

05 Bot chien
Fried cubes of rice-flour dough bound by egg and topped with green onions, served over shredded green papaya.

06 Bun thit nuong
Chargrilled pork tops rice noodles, lettuce and herbs, with peanuts and a fish sauce dressing.

07 Bo la lot
Grilled beef wrapped in fragrant betel leaves and rolled up in rice paper.

08 Hu tieu

This clear noodle soup with slices of pork and shrimp goes great with *hoanh thanh* (wontons).

09 Pho

Saigon's answer to the classic noodle soup is sweeter and grittier than the Hanoi version. Ask for *dac biet* to get the works.

10 Com ga xoi mo

The closest thing to local fried chicken you'll find, a marinated drumstick or thigh sits atop fried rice with a small side salad.

11 Bo ne

A mix of thinly cut steak, pâté, pork sausage, sliced onions and an egg, all delivered on a sizzling cast-iron plate.

12 Banh cuon

These steamed sheets of rice flour envelop a de-licious filling of minced pork and mushrooms.

13 Com tam

Grilled pork chop, chewy pork skin, savoury quiche and a fried egg served over broken rice with sweet and salty fish sauce drizzled on top.

42

The Craft-Beer
SCENE

BEER | DRINKING | FOOD

The city's craft-beer scene has been booming since the mid-2010s, with dozens of breweries concocting delicious varieties of beer with distinctly Vietnamese flavours. While the Vietnamese drink about 4.4 billion L of beer annually, it's usually with the view of getting tipsy quickly. Craft beer has turned that notion on its head, encouraging the savouring of some superb offerings.

JAMES PHAM/LONELY PLANET ©

📷 How to

Where to drink Most craft-beer taprooms are located in downtown Districts 1 and 3, with some popping up in the expat enclave of District 2. Check out the Ho Chi Minh City Ale Trail (download the map from its Facebook site), a selection of some of the best-known taprooms, and the countrywide map of craft-beer establishments from craftbeer vietnam.com.

Budget buster Local beer can be cheaper than bottled water in Vietnam, but craft beer can be around five times as much, so budget accordingly.

JEAST WEST BREWING CO ©

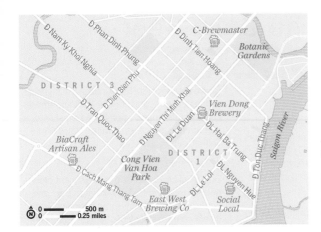

Top left BiaCraft Artisan Ales **Bottom left** East West Brewing Co

Vien Dong Brewery Established in 1995, home-grown and family-owned Vien Dong Brewery is known for experimenting with everything from coconut and passion fruit to naturally fermented persimmons from Dalat and even pine needles. Try the Bay craft lager made from a mash of wheat and sticky rice, or the Lambic-style Leo Leo with hints of orange peel, coriander and peppercorns, available at **Social Local**.

C-Brewmaster With breweries in Hanoi and Tien Giang (tours available), Vietnamese-owned C-Brewmaster has more than 50 ales, lagers, Pilsners, stouts and IPAs to choose from, along with a dozen ciders. More than half are inspired by Vietnamese flavours, like the Warrior Sisters Pilsner lager with notes of mandarin and the Acerola Cherry cider made from 100% raw materials from Tien Giang.

East West Brewing Co Saigon's first in-house craft brewery and kitchen concept, East West serves up its foundation craft beer in a large, airy industrial-inspired downtown taproom featuring an extensive menu of Vietnamese bites traditionally eaten with beer. Wash it all down with the Loc-Ness Monster, aged in bourbon oak barrels and one of the strongest beers made in Vietnam (20% ABV).

BiaCraft Artisan Ales To sample craft beer from all over Vietnam, head to BiaCraft's District 3 taproom, where you'll find the city's most extensive selection, including 50 beers on tap with an additional 200 or so in the fridge. The brewery also has its own line of hilariously and irreverently named craft beer like the Ugly But Vain with notes of grapefruit and passion fruit.

Pairing
// Vietnamese Food with Craft Beer

Pair up a stout with rich, braised foods like caramelised pork and shrimp.

A spicy noodle dish like *bun thit nuong* matches beautifully with malty amber ales.

When eating a pomelo and seafood salad, bust out a wheat beer to complement the citrusy flavours.

IPAs and pale ales can serve as a great accompaniment to rich *pho bo* (beef noodle soup) or BBQ meats such as goat breast.

Don't forget, a crisp, clean lager or blonde is going to let snails and freshly grilled seafood shine.

■ Recommended by **Tim Scott,** *founder of BiaCraft Artisan Ales* @biacraftartisanales

Listings

BEST OF THE REST

See & Do

Saigon Street Eats

Created by Australian-Vietnamese couple Barbara and Vu, these fun small-group tours are an excellent entry into Ho Chi Minh City's food scene, with lots of interesting stories including deep dives into *pho* and seafood.

Urban Adventures

Urban Adventures offers several tours but the *cyclo* (pedicab) tour is especially fun, as you get to visit a few main attractions from the back of a vintage *cyclo,* including time to sample a drip coffee and a bowl of *pho*.

Old Compass Travel

Get underneath the skin of Ho Chi Minh City with these small-group tours, which showcase insider stories of the city's architecture, culture, religion, history and food in a fun, engaging manner.

Les Rives

Everything is more fun on a speedboat, as Les Rives shows on its tours to Cu Chi, the Mekong Delta, Can Gio, as well as around Ho Chi Minh City itself. Guides are personable, and the river element is delightful.

Meals with a View

Blank Lounge $$

Some of the best views of the city can be had at Blank Lounge on floors 75 and 76 of the city's tallest building, Landmark 81. Grab a seat on the outside terrace in time for sunset with a cocktail and canapé.

Propaganda $$

Come for the colourful murals in the style of propaganda art, and stay for the Vietnamese comfort food made using the freshest of ingredients, all across from the Notre Dame Cathedral.

42 ĐL Nguyen Hue $

Built in the mid-1960s, this apartment block now houses over two dozen cafes, bars and boutiques. After doing some shopping, grab a seat on the balcony of one of the cafes and people-watch over ĐL Nguyen Hue walking street.

Secret Garden $$

Walk up the stairs of an old apartment building on Đ Pasteur to get to the rooftop Secret Garden, where everything on its extensive menu is a winner, spanning cuisines from all of Vietnam's main regions.

Drink Vietnam

Shri Restaurant & Lounge $$$

Located 23 storeys above the city, Shri serves up excellent European fare, but it's

42 ĐL Nguyen Hue

the amazing cocktails inspired by Saigon that you'll want to sample. Also look for the whisky room hidden behind a sliding bookcase.

Firkin Bar $$$

Long and narrow in dark wood and leather seats, Firkin Bar has a sophisticated yet cosy vibe. The highlight here is definitely the bespoke whisky-forward cocktails made just for you from the 400 or so bottles of liquor on hand.

Cuisine with a Quirk

Villa Royale Antiques & Tea Room $$

Sit down to homemade European comfort food and decadent desserts surrounded by one-of-a-kind antiques in this beautiful home about 20 minutes from District 1. There's even a small pool for when the Saigon heat is too much to bear.

Quince Eatery $$$

Fine dining in a contemporary, casual setting makes this a Saigon favourite for its excellent Mediterranean and produce-driven fare, mostly cooked over an oven fire-grill in the open kitchen.

R House Diner & Lounge $$

R House partners with local shelters to help find homes for abandoned, traumatised dogs. Enjoy mostly vegan and vegetarian versions of international comfort food while interacting with dogs awaiting their new homes, if you like.

Noir $$

Put your taste buds to the test as you try and figure out what you're eating completely in the dark. Flavoursome menus feature various cuisines from around Vietnam, Asia and the world, but you won't know exactly what you've had until after. Hosts are mainly blind or visually impaired.

Cyclo tour

A Piece of Saigon

Loui Tobias

Leave Ho Chi Minh City with a portrait by British artist Loui Tobias; the works are very reasonably priced. Married to a Vietnamese woman, Loui is often inspired by neighbours and other locals.

Saigon Kitsch

A one-stop souvenir shop with artsy but also functional mementos, including notebooks, mugs and bags. The propaganda posters and items made from recycled rice bags are big hits with shoppers.

Dominique Saint Paul

Skip the conical hat and instead pick up a pair of gorgeous custom leather shoes handmade in Vietnam using European techniques. Pre-order on the website or come for a fitting at the shop and have them delivered internationally. A limited number of ready-to-wear shoes and accessories available on site.

 Scan to find more things to do in Ho Chi Minh City online

MEKONG DELTA

CULTURE | CRUISING | COUNTRY LIFE

Experience
the Mekong
Delta online

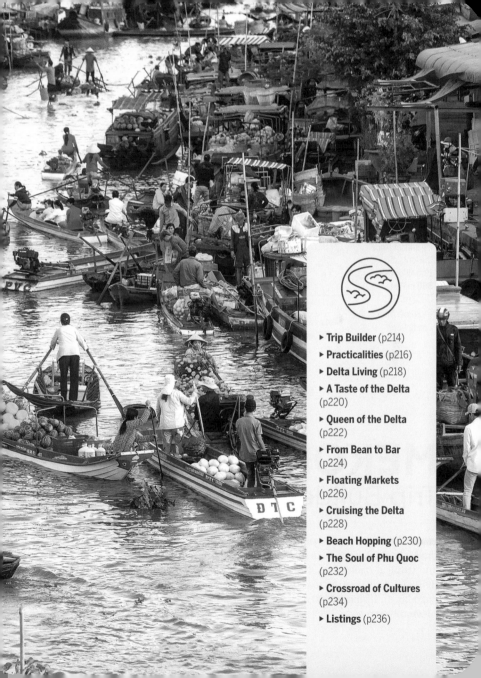

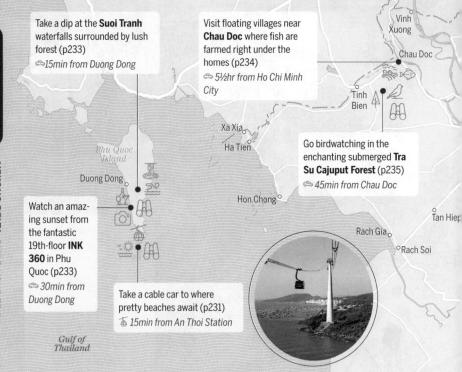

Take a dip at the **Suoi Tranh** waterfalls surrounded by lush forest (p233)
🚗 15min from Duong Dong

Visit floating villages near **Chau Doc** where fish are farmed right under the homes (p234)
🚗 5½hr from Ho Chi Minh City

Go birdwatching in the enchanting submerged **Tra Su Cajuput Forest** (p235)
🚗 45min from Chau Doc

Watch an amazing sunset from the fantastic 19th-floor **INK 360** in Phu Quoc (p233)
🚗 30min from Duong Dong

Take a cable car to where pretty beaches await (p231)
🚠 15min from An Thoi Station

Vinh Xuong

Chau Doc

Tinh Bien

Xa Xia

Ha Tien

Phu Quoc Island

Duong Dong

Hon Chong

Tan Hiep

Rach Gia

Rach Soi

Gulf of Thailand

Ca Mau

Cai Nuoc

Nam Can

MEKONG DELTA
Trip Builder

Criss-crossed by countless rivers and canals, the Mekong Delta is blanketed by emerald rice fields and tropical-fruit farms. Immerse yourself in country living with its floating markets, ethnic-minority pagodas and friendly villages, before mass tourism inevitably arrives.

Explore bookable experiences on the Mekong Delta

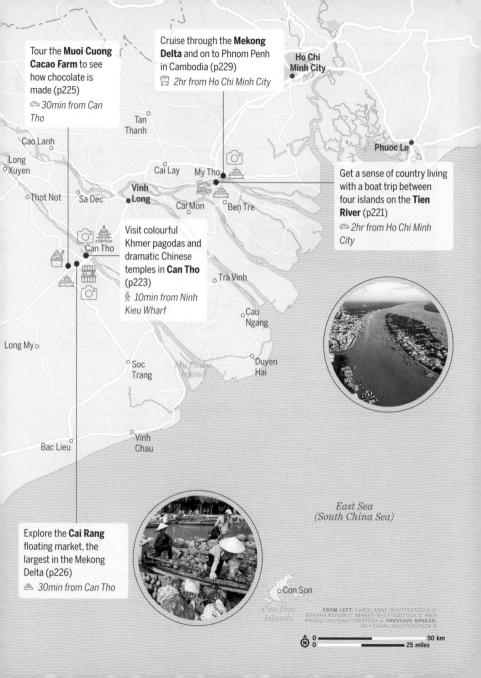

Tour the **Muoi Cuong Cacao Farm** to see how chocolate is made (p225)

🚐 *30min from Can Tho*

Cruise through the **Mekong Delta** and on to Phnom Penh in Cambodia (p229)

🚌 *2hr from Ho Chi Minh City*

Ho Chi Minh City

Tan Thanh

Cao Lanh

Long Xuyen

Cai Lay   My Tho

Thot Not   Sa Dec

Vinh Long

Cai Mon   Ben Tre

Phuoc Le

Get a sense of country living with a boat trip between four islands on the **Tien River** (p221)

🚐 *2hr from Ho Chi Minh City*

Visit colourful Khmer pagodas and dramatic Chinese temples in **Can Tho** (p223)

🚶 *10min from Ninh Kieu Wharf*

Can Tho

Tra Vinh

Cau Ngang

Long My

Soc Trang

My Phuoc Island

Duyen Hai

Bac Lieu

Vinh Chau

East Sea (South China Sea)

Explore the **Cai Rang** floating market, the largest in the Mekong Delta (p226)

⛴ *30min from Can Tho*

Con Son

Con Dao Islands

Ⓝ 0 ———————— 50 km
0 ———————— 25 miles

Practicalities

VIVANVU/SHUTTERSTOCK ©

ARRIVING

Phu Quoc International Airport Located 10km southeast of the main town of Duong Dong. Ferries arrive on the east coast of the island from Ha Tien and Rach Gia.

Can Tho International Airport Lies 10km north-west of the city centre, serving a handful of domestic destinations and fewer international ones.

Other destinations in the Mekong Delta are served by buses and shuttles from Ho Chi Minh City and elsewhere, including Phnom Penh in Cambodia.

HOW MUCH FOR A

Phu Quoc tour
600,000d

boat to Cai Rang
floating market
50,000d

My Tho noodle soup
35,000d

WHEN TO GO

DEC–FEB
Ideal time to visit, with cool temperatures and sunny skies.

MAR–MAY
Rising temperatures and humidity, but still pleasant.

JUN–AUG
Start of rainy season with short, heavy showers.

SEP–NOV
Temperatures start to cool as rain tapers off in November.

GETTING AROUND

Renting a motorbike Smaller towns in the Mekong Delta are ideal for exploring by motorbike, even for novice drivers, with plenty of quiet lanes to putter along. However, highways in between towns are heavily trafficked with large trucks.

Taxis Taxis are a good option, as are motorbike taxis for short trips. On Phu Quoc, fares in between town and the beaches in the north and south of the island are relatively expensive due to the distance – something to keep in mind if you're staying outside Duong Dong.

Boating Boats in major tourist spots will have a join-in option. Otherwise, ask your hotel to help arrange a charter and itinerary.

EATING & DRINKING

Called the 'rice bowl of Vietnam' for its bounty, the Mekong Delta produces a cornucopia of rice, fruit and seafood, meaning its specialities are based on super-fresh ingredients. Tropical fruit from the market is always a winner, as are the many types of soups, including hotpots. Many have broth made from pickled fish (called *mam*); while the pungent flavour takes some getting used to, it's rich and soul-satisfying. The delta version of *banh xeo* (pictured bottom left), a sizzling crêpe wrapped up with fresh herbs, is delicious.

Best cocktail with views

INK 360, Phu Quoc (p233)

Must-try noodle soup

Cai Rang floating market (p226)

MONEY

Few places take plastic, so be prepared with cash. Your main expenses in the delta will be transport and tours. Expect everything to cost slightly more on Phu Quoc, especially Western food.

CONNECT & FIND YOUR WAY

Wi-fi Hotels, guesthouses and fancy cafes will usually have wi-fi, but don't expect it from small roadside eateries. Having a data plan is handy throughout most of the delta.

Navigation Google Maps works well in the delta, except for barely-there country roads. Don't get too worried about getting lost; friendly locals can point you back to the main road.

WHERE TO STAY

Cheap, family-run guesthouses are plentiful throughout the Mekong Delta with a few upscale properties in the larger cities. Phu Quoc has a superb range of options.

Place	Pros/Cons
Ben Tre	Đ Dong Khoi and Đ Hung Vuong are centrally located to restaurants and markets.
Can Tho	Anywhere near the riverside; Can Tho Market is close to the action.
Chau Doc	The riverfront is the city's main attraction, so start looking here.
My Tho	Look into homestays set on farmlands or river islands to experience country living. Expect rustic conditions.
Phu Quoc	Backed by restaurants and bars, Long Beach can feel hectic. Ong Lang Beach (north) offers quiet seclusion, but it'll cost you.

PROTECT YOURSELF

Visiting the Mekong Delta means lots of outdoor activities, so stay hydrated and bring a hat. Avoid doing too much during the hottest part of the day.

Delta Living

LIFE IN THE 'RICE BOWL OF VIETNAM'

Known as the 'rice bowl of Vietnam', the Mekong Delta is all about farming and fishing. Life is slow here, measured by the rise and fall of the river and the planting and harvesting of crops. While the joys are simple, this pastoral life is increasingly under threat.

It goes by many names after it springs from the Himalaya: Lancang Jiang (meaning 'turbulent river') as it makes its way through China, on to Myanmar and Laos, and then Thailand where it's known as the Mae Kong or Mae Nam Kong (meaning 'mother water'). After flowing through Cambodia, the Mekong River finishes its 4500km-long journey in Vietnam's Mekong Delta, where it's known as Song Cuu Long, or 'river of the nine dragons', splitting into nine branches before finally emptying out into the sea.

Considered the world's most productive river, the Mekong brings life to Vietnam's Mekong Delta, a vast area of over 40,000 sq km and home to more than 21 million people. With over 28,000km of rivers and canals criss-crossing the land like arteries and vessels, pumping water used for irrigation, transport, food, aquaculture and, of course, bathing and cooking, water is life.

It's said the map of Vietnam looks like two rice baskets connected by a yoke, pointing to the fertile Red River Delta in the north and the Mekong Delta in the south. But it's the Mekong Delta, where more than 80% of the population is engaged in rice farming, that does the heavy lifting, responsible for producing more than half of Vietnam's rice and two-thirds of the country's fruit.

Everywhere you go in the delta, you see people living on, by and near the water. 'We have cool breezes all day. It's clean, not dusty like on land,' says Oanh, whose family lives aboard a boat on the Chau Doc River. 'We can move our boat wherever we want along the river.'

The boat has all the conveniences of home, such as potted plants and a small satellite dish for the television. Electricity

Left Rice harvesting **Middle** Boats, Mekong River **Right** Farmer irrigating crops

is supplied by a line from shore, and a pump brings in river water, which must be boiled before drinking or using to cook.

But it's what's under the houseboat, buoyed by plastic barrels, that really ties the family to the river. Oanh lifts up a wooden panel on the floor and, immediately, there's a loud thrashing of 150,000 hungry fish waiting to be fed. Like many of the floating houses on the river, Oanh farms fish in large pens underneath, taking advantage of the nutrients and currents of the river.

> Oanh lifts up a wooden panel on the floor and, immediately, there's a loud thrashing of 150,000 hungry fish waiting to be fed.

Her husband and son work at grinding up a concoction of sea fish, rice and potatoes to feed the voracious eaters for eight to 10 months before they're ready for market. 'Sometimes we hear them thrashing at night. That means they're not getting enough oxygen because the river isn't flowing fast enough. Then we have to get up and turn on the motor to create a current for them.'

It's a difficult way to make a living. The family outlays 2.5 billion dong (US$115,000) per season, with no guarantees that the fish will even survive to maturity or what the market price will be when they're ready for sale. 'It's a hard life and I'd rather my children go to school and work in an office, without the risks and worries of living on the water. On the other hand, because we live right here above the fish, our family is always together. Whatever we lack in money, we make up for with love,' she says with a smile.

The Delta's Uncertain Future

While the simplicity of the delta may seem idyllic, there are increasing dangers to this languid way of life so dependent on water. Climate change and rising sea levels put the low-lying delta in jeopardy, with reports predicting that a sizeable area will be flooded by 2030. Salinity intrusion caused by a decline in rainfall and reduced river flow from upstream dams means that farmers, ironically, have to buy fresh water to irrigate crops and for everyday living. Interestingly, the signs on the boats that sell water read 'exchange water', as the word for 'water' *(nuoc)* can also mean 'country', so 'selling water' can also be interpreted as 'selling your country' or 'treason'.

43 TASTE
of the Delta

COUNTRY LIVING | BIRDWATCHING | BOATING

▬▬▬ Just two hours southeast of Ho Chi Minh City are the sister cities of My Tho and Ben Tre, on opposite sides of the river and gateway to the Mekong Delta. Leave the urban jungle behind and immerse yourself in country living with scenic boat rides along rivers and canals, exploring how people live close to nature and seeing how local materials are turned into handicrafts and food products.

HIEN PHUNG THU/SHUTTERSTOCK ©

🗺 How to

Getting here Buses and minivans make the two-hour journey from Ho Chi Minh City a breeze. My Tho and Ben Tre are close to each other, so taxis are the best way to travel between them.

Cruising Most overnight cruises through the Mekong Delta depart from My Tho. Consider arriving a day or two early to explore the area at your leisure before boarding.

What to buy Anything made from coconut (oil, candy, kitchen utensils), and tasty snacks like *nem* (pickled pork) and *banh trang chuoi* (rice paper embedded with banana slices).

ANTON_IVANOV/SHUTTERSTOCK ©

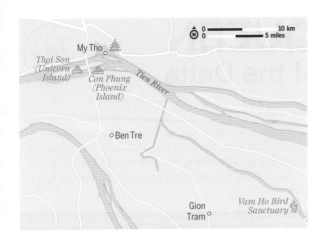

Top left Con Phung **Bottom left** Vinh Trang Pagoda

River islands On the Tien River between My Tho and Ben Tre are four river islands named after animals in Vietnamese mythology. Boat cruises reveal slices of countryside life: workshops making coconut candy and other local products, fruit orchards and honey farms. **Thoi Son (Unicorn Island)** has a tourist centre which offers horse-carriage rides along village paths, boat rides through palm-fringed canals, and fruit sampling accompanied by traditional folk-music performances. On **Con Phung (Phoenix Island)**, there is a raucously coloured temple dedicated to the Coconut Monk who founded a sect blending Buddhism, Christianity, Hinduism and a lifestyle based on eating only coconuts.

Big Buddha Theravada Buddhism was first introduced to the Mekong Delta in the 4th century CE, likely through ethnic Khmer adherents. In My Tho, the pretty **Vinh Trang Pagoda** is home to more than 60 Buddha statues of wood and bronze, including three giant Buddhas (lying, standing and sitting). After strolling the landscaped grounds, stop for a *hu tieu My Tho*, a noodle soup featuring clear, chewy noodles and a rich broth made from simmering pork bones and dried seafood.

Go birding Just outside Ben Tre is the 40-hectare **Vam Ho Bird Sanctuary**, home to 84 species of birds including 500,000 storks. Set by the Ba Lai River, the sanctuary is densely forested by nipa palms and mangroves – a gorgeous setting for quiet late-afternoon boat rides and guided walks as the birds come back to roost. Next door is a tourist centre offering handicraft workshops and walks through the fruit orchards.

🏃 Get Lost!

Perhaps better than any single attraction is simply wandering the lanes and villages of the Mekong Delta. You'll stumble upon pastoral landscapes and people going about their business, most of them completely unbothered by tourism. You'll come across authentic vignettes of local life, such as small country markets and home workshops making everything from rice paper to bricks the traditional way or villagers weaving palm fronds into new roofs. Get outside the urban centres and randomly veer down small paved paths that lead to hamlets and villages. There are always roads that lead back out, even without the help of Google Maps, so don't worry – just get lost!

44 QUEEN
of the Delta

CULTURE | CUISINE | ARCHITECTURE

━━━ Known as Vietnam's 'Western capital', Can Tho is the largest city in the Mekong Delta, just about a four-hour drive from Ho Chi Minh City. With its many universities and employment opportunities, it draws people from all over the delta along with their regional dishes, beliefs and subcultures, making Can Tho a fascinating destination.

JET HUYNH CAN/GETTY IMAGES ©

📖 How to

Getting here Can Tho is about 170km southwest of Ho Chi Minh City; the bus ride takes less than four hours. The city also has an airport servicing several domestic destinations as well as budget flights to Bangkok and Kuala Lumpur.

Walking tour Downtown Can Tho is very compact, with the excellent Can Tho Museum, Ninh Kieu Pier and its 7.2m-high statue of Ho Chi Minh, the historic Can Tho Market, Ong Temple and more all within a 10-minute walking radius.

HUY THOAI/SHUTTERSTOCK ©

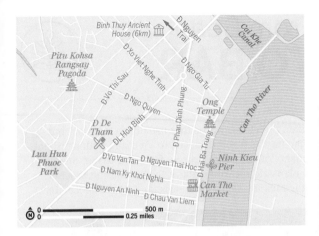

Top left Binh Thuy Ancient House
Bottom left Ninh Kieu Pier

River views More than the place to catch a boat to the Cai Rang floating market, the **Ninh Kieu Pier** is synonymous with Can Tho. Find a stone bench under shady trees to watch the river go by at this pretty riverside park. Remember to come back later for sunset views and to browse the vibrant night market here or at the **Can Tho Market** (built in 1915) just a block away.

Period architecture If you saw the 1992 movie *The Lover,* based on the book by Marguerite Duras, the **Binh Thuy Ancient House** may look familiar. Finished in 1911, the home is a notable example of early-20th-century French and Asian architectural elements with its colonial-era tiles, vintage furnishings and ornately carved screens and statues.

Temples and pagodas Can Tho's mix of cultures extends to its impressive religious sites. The Khmer people worship at the photogenic **Pitu Khosa Rangsay Pagoda**, where dragons, fairies, birds and deities adorn its three gilded levels. The colourful **Ong Temple** (completed in 1896) was once the Guangzhou Assembly Hall, a place for Chinese immigrants to worship and socialise.

Delta delights While Can Tho doesn't really have a dish all its own, it draws cuisine from the region like *bun mam,* a fish noodle soup from Soc Trang province made from pickled fish (it tastes better than it sounds), and the Khmer-influenced *banh cong* – fried muffin-like rice-flour cakes topped with shrimp. Head to the local foodie street of **Đ De Tham** and eat your way through a host of Mekong Delta specialities.

☆ Hidden Highlights of Can Tho

Fruit farms on Son islet
Sample organic longans, rambutans, mangosteens and more, fresh off the branch.

Cycling around Can Tho
Feast your eyes on scenes of mango trees, dragon-fruit plants and green fields of rice.

Sau Hoai noodle factory
Near the Cai Rang floating market, try your hand at steaming the delicate rice paper and cutting it up into noodles.

Gian Gua relic site See a gua tree that's more than 150 years old – with solid branches and roots intertwining into a dense canopy – while listening to stories of how Can Tho residents fought through wars with both the French and Americans.

■ **Recommended by Vo Minh Trung,**
tour supervisor
at Victoria Can Tho Resort
@victoria.cantho

45 From Bean
TO BAR

CHOCOLATE | FARMING | CULTURE

Chocolate and Vietnam aren't two words that usually go together, but in the last few decades cacao has been reintroduced to Vietnam, with artisanal chocolate makers taking charge of the entire process from pod to bar. Spend an hour or two on a cacao plantation learning about the fascinating process, including how the soil of the Mekong Delta influences the taste of chocolate.

LEQUANGNHUT/SHUTTERSTOCK ©

📖 How to

Getting here Cacao farms are mostly unmarked, as cacao is grown together with other crops. Most of the farmers don't speak English, so you should seek out the ones that offer tours, like those mentioned opposite.

What to buy Products for sale in most cases are a fraction of what they would be in stores. Cacao nibs, considered a superfood, are a good buy. Cacao juice and wine, made in limited quantities, are delicious.

When to go Harvesting season is typically March to May and October to December, but the farms can be visited year-round.

JAMES PHAM/LONELY PLANET ©

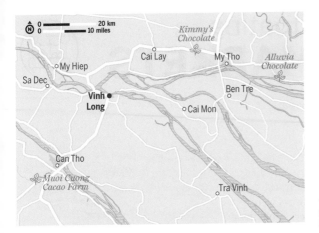

Top left Processing cacao **Bottom left** Cacao pod, Muoi Cuong Cacao Farm

Muoi Cuong Cacao Farm Just a 30-minute drive from Can Tho, Mr Cuong has grown cacao for over half a century, with 2000 or so cacao trees on his 1.2-hectare plot. Tour the plantation to see the rudimentary machines used to process cacao, including a wood-burning hand roaster. His small-scale operation produces chocolate bars, cocoa powder and roasted cacao nibs – if you ask nicely, he may even share a glass of homemade cacao wine, a tartly sweet, lightly alcoholic drink made from the flesh of the cacao fruit.

Kimmy's Chocolate Named after the owner's wife, Kimmy's Chocolate (kimmychocolatier.com) started as a way of helping the neighbours generate income from growing cacao. Just outside My Tho, the spotless home factory churns out small quantities of cocoa powder, cocoa butter, chocolate bars and a decadent chocolate-cashew spread. While there are no cacao trees on site, tours of the factory reveal the fascinating bean-to-bar process, including the addition of local ingredients like red pepper, ginger and cashews.

Alluvia Chocolate The chocolate supplier to Jetstar Airlines, Alluvia Chocolate (alluviachocolate.com) offers weekend tours from Ho Chi Minh City to their factory in Cho Gao, about two hours away. Visitors can tour the cacao farm, learn how the beans are harvested, fermented and roasted before being turned into chocolate, and even mould and package a small keepsake bar of chocolate. Their single-origin chocolate highlights the fruity notes that the delta's alluvial soil infuses into the finished product.

⚖ Coconut & Cacao

Introduced to Vietnam by the French in the late 1800s, cacao initially didn't take off as a cash crop. However, the industry was revived in the early 2000s when organisations like USAID provided thousands of farmers with seedlings, fertiliser, as well as training to grow cacao using sustainable cropping practices. The plan took off, in part because cacao trees can be intercropped or grown together with existing coconut trees, which are plentiful in the Mekong Delta, offering farmers a way to harvest additional crops year-round without the need for more land. Different soil types even impart a distinct flavour to the beans.

46 Floating MARKETS

MARKETS | CULTURE | BOATING

▬▬▬ The floating markets of the Mekong Delta are a century-old tradition from a time when travel and trade along the waterways were cheaper, safer and more accessible than by road. Barges laden down with fruit, vegetables and rice sell their products wholesale to smaller boats for resale at land-based markets. They're fun, busy and colourful, but fast disappearing.

🗺 How to

Getting here Floating markets are usually found near large junctions in the river, close to larger land-based markets. Rowboats usually ferry customers across the river or, at the larger markets, give tours to tourists. Expect to pay 300,000d to 500,000d to charter a boat for 10 to 12 people, or wait until the boat fills up and pay 30,000d to 50,000d per person.

When to go While some boats stay all day, floating markets are busiest in early mornings, from about 5am to 8am.

There are about a dozen noteworthy floating markets throughout the delta, each with its own personality. If you're not planning a long foray into the delta, the 20 or so boats that make up the floating market at **Cai Be** are the closest to Ho Chi Minh City (about a three-hour drive). Its easy accessibility means it gets a lot of bus groups and is well set up for tourists. As a wholesale hub, it's busiest early in the morning and late at night.

For the delta's biggest floating market, head to **Cai Rang**, 6km from Can Tho. While you can drive to the

Top right Fruit sellers, Mekong Delta **Bottom right** Victoria Can Tho Resort

⛵ For Sale

The long poles on each boat, with produce attached at the top, let people know what that boat has for sale. Roofing material shows that the boat itself is for sale.

market and hire one of the waiting boats nearby, a more scenic option is taking the 30-minute boat ride from Can Tho's Ninh Kieu Pier. If you're feeling extra fancy, **Victoria Can Tho Resort** and **Azerai Can Tho** offer breakfast cruises to the floating market, typically with a stop on the way back at one of the local workshops.

Heading further south, you'll come across the less touristy floating markets of **Tra On** (Vinh Long province; busiest when the tides come in), **Nga Bay** (also known as Phung Hiep, in Hau Giang province), and the busy **Nga Nam** (Soc Trang province). Situated at the junction of five rivers, the narrow section of the river bunches the boats closer together, creating a lively atmosphere.

CRUISING
the Delta

CRUISING | RIVER LIFE | HANDICRAFTS

With thousands of kilometres of waterways, seeing the Mekong Delta by cruise is a no-brainer. In addition to the unique perspective, shore excursions are usually varied, with lots to see because so much activity takes place on and by the water. As a bonus, enjoy a break from planning since food, accommodation and activities are usually included.

ROMAN BABAKIN/SHUTTERSTOCK ©

How to

Planning your cruise
For day cruises, you'll often find tourist boats stationed near major river attractions like floating markets and by urban ports like Can Tho's Ninh Kieu Pier. In smaller communities, there are often small boats ferrying people across the river.

But you can negotiate to charter the boat based on duration and distance. If you're a nervous cruiser, opt for larger boats that sit higher in the water.

Save time Maximise your time by choosing a one-way cruise ending in Rach Gia (jumping-off point for Phu Quoc) or Phnom Penh, Cambodia.

BLUESKY85/GETTY IMAGES ©

ULLSTEIN BILD/GETTY IMAGES ©

Far left Nighttime cruise, Can Tho
Bottom left Mat weaving **Near left** Inside a cruise boat

Day cruises Hands down the best way to experience a floating market or one of the delta's riverine islands is by day cruise, whether it's joining other travellers on a tourist boat or hiring a canoe all for yourself. Be aware that short cruises can feel inauthentic and rushed from trying to pack too many activities into a very short window, not to mention the travel time to and from your cruise starting point. A pricey but time-maximising option is a speedboat cruise from Ho Chi Minh City by **Les Rives** (lesrivesexperience.com).

Overnight journeys If you can, try to spend at least one night on the water to experience how the villages quieten down at night and get going very early in the morning. Overnight journeys also have the advantage of sailing further away from the most touristed attractions. You'll also have more time to interact with the crew, many of whom are from the delta.

Multi-day sailings Sailing from Vietnam's Mekong Delta to Cambodia's capital of Phnom Penh, or even to Siem Reap (gateway to Angkor Wat), can really be a spectacular way to explore the Mekong River, offering so much more to see than the rather bland overland route. While most multi-day cruises leave from near My Tho (closer to Ho Chi Minh City), consider ones that sail the less touristed southern arm of the Mekong River from Can Tho, such as **Victoria Mekong Cruises** (p237).

Handicrafts from the Mekong Delta

With a lot of downtime in between rice harvests, the people of the Mekong Delta are used to making things on the side. Together with an abundance of natural resources found locally, one of the highlights of cruise shore excursions is seeing how home-based workshops turn out an impressive array of products, most of it by hand. For instance, the wood from coconut palms can be carved into utensils, the leaves can be woven into thatched panels for roofing or walls, and the coconut flesh turned into candy. Common handicrafts include mats woven from water hyacinth, bamboo and woodcarving, and incense sticks made from wood dust.

48 Beach
HOPPING

BEACHES | DIVING | ISLANDS

━━━ With 150km of coastline, Phu Quoc has nearly two dozen beaches to discover – from busy Long Beach right in town, packed with restaurants and beach clubs, to blissfully remote spots that require an adventurous motorbike ride down dirt paths.

JOERG FRIEDL/SHUTTERSTOCK ©

📷 How to

Getting around To best explore the beaches at your own pace, consider renting a motorbike for the day. The island's main roads are relatively easy to navigate, but be careful on sandy paths and remember to stock up on petrol if driving through the national park.

When to visit October to March has dry, sunny days, while June to October sees a 50/50 chance of monsoonal rains.

Travel packages Check domestic airline websites for money-saving combos of flights and hotel.

DREAMARCHITECT/SHUTTERSTOCK ©

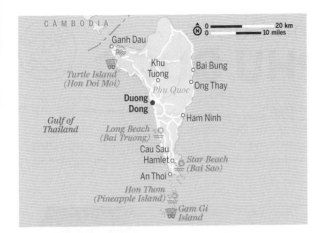

Top left Uninhabited island near Phu Quoc **Bottom left** Ganh Dau

Top Snorkelling Spots

Turtle Island (Hon Doi Moi) north side Large vibrant coral-reef heads just below the surface and shallow underwater canyons at just a few metres' depth.

Turtle Island (Hon Doi Moi) south side Patches of anemones with their resident pink skunk clownfish are found here, along with nudibranch and other colourful fish.

Kim Quy Rock outcropping dominates the ocean topography here, with butterfly fish, wrasses and a variety of soft and hard corals.

Lighthouse Protected from currents, this relaxing place to snorkel is home to a very large colony of anemones.

Gam Gi Island An area of soft and hard corals and home to a large variety of fish species.

■ Recommended by Jeremy P Stein, *PADI course director and founder of Rainbow Divers–Vietnam @jezza.vn*

Star Beach (Bai Sao) Named after the starfish that once came up in droves, this is one of the island's prettiest beaches, with white powder sand, clear turquoise water and swaying palm trees. Get there early, before the afternoon tour buses arrive, and stake out your spot at one of the beach clubs or restaurants.

Pineapple paradise Hop aboard the world's longest nonstop three-rope cable car for the 20-minute ride to **Hon Thom (Pineapple Island)** and take in the sweeping sea views. The golden-sand beach is gorgeous, but you can also pay a bit more to enjoy the on-site water park and buffet restaurant.

Fishing-village vibes The northwestern tip of the island isn't just the closest point to the Cambodian islands; it's also blissfully (as yet) undeveloped, centred around the fishing village of **Ganh Dau**. Hire a boat and snorkel the waters around the two off-islands of **Bang** and **Thay Boi**, come for lunch and a dip in the pool at **Gold Coast Resort**, or enjoy a seafood feast at **Bien Hai Quan**.

Long Beach (Bai Truong) True to its name, this 20km-long beach on the southwestern side of the island stretches from Duong Dong all the way south. Closer to town, the palm-fringed beach is lined with hotels and restaurants. Halfway down, the **Phu Quoc Marina** has a nice selection of upscale restaurants, beach clubs and hotels.

49 The Soul of PHU QUOC

WATERFALLS | SUNSETS | SEAFOOD

▬▬ Spend a day discovering what else – other than beautiful beaches – Phu Quoc has to offer, including swimming under a waterfall, feasting on (literally) sea-to-table seafood, and catching the famed Phu Quoc sunset from the highest point on the island.

FOKUSGOOD/SHUTTERSTOCK ©

🗺 Trip Notes

Getting around While some of these sights are included in tours of northern Phu Quoc, it's easy to drive along main roads or negotiate a rate for a half- or full-day taxi.

Phu Quoc pepper The island's soil yields its distinctive pepper with a sweet, citrusy heat. In addition to using it dry, many restaurants in Phu Quoc add fresh strands of peppercorns to dishes.

Forest walk Over half the island is a national park. For the most accessible trail from Duong Dong, take the well-worn path after the 5km Ganh Dau road marker.

🥣 Pearls & Pepper

Although a tiny island, Phu Quoc has a few signature products famous across Vietnam and beyond, including black pepper (pictured), fish sauce, cultured pearls and *sim* wine, a sweet liqueur made from wild berries. There are small factories all over the island where you can see the fascinating process of making these products.

Ganh Dau
(16km)

01 Get up early to arrive before the crowds for a refreshing dip in the pretty **Suoi Tranh** waterfalls, set among sculpture gardens and landscaped grounds and surrounded by forest.

Duong
Dong

03 The **Thanh Nga Sanctuary** showcases what the muscular, intelligent Phu Quoc ridgeback (one of only three varieties in the world) can do, including scaling tall fences.

Ham Ninh

02 Pick your own seafood at the **Ham Ninh** fishing village from baskets submerged in the sea. Go for a local breakfast of rice congee with seafood, or have a feast cooked up the way you want.

Gulf of
Thailand

04 Spend the day lazing by the pool or beach at **Sailing Club Phu Quoc**, supplied by smoothies and cocktails from the swim-up bar and upscale versions of international comfort food.

05 Phu Quoc has some of the prettiest sunsets in Vietnam. The terrace of **INK 360**, on the 19th floor of the InterContinental, is the island's best vantage point.

Cau Sau
Hamlet

ORIANA LUDOLINI/SHUTTERSTOCK ©

N
0   5 km
0   2.5 miles

50 Crossroad of
CULTURES

BOATING | NATURE | CULTURE

━━━━ While most people only overnight in Chau Doc on the way between Phnom Penh in Cambodia and Ho Chi Minh City, there's actually a lot to see in this border town by the river. Stay an extra night or two to explore life lived on the river, or visit communities and religious sites reflecting Khmer, Cham and Chinese influences.

🗺 How to

Getting here Chau Doc is about 220km by bus from Ho Chi Minh City and 140km by boat from Phnom Penh, Cambodia.

When to go September to November is the rainy season but also the best time to visit the Tra Su Cajuput Forest, when water levels are highest.

Must-try The *bun ca Chau Doc,* a fish noodle soup tinged with turmeric and flavoured with pickled fish, a speciality of the Mekong Delta.

CAMBODIA
Floating Market
Chau Doc
Lady Xu Temple
Vinh Te Canal
Sam Mountain
Phnom Den
Tinh Bien
Tra Su Cajuput Forest
Tuc Dup Hill
Tri Ton
0 10 km
0 5 miles

Boating Situated where the Chau Doc River, Bassac River and Vinh Te Canal meet, Chau Doc is best explored by boat. Boat trips visit the nearby floating market as well as the floating fish farms, pens built under the houses buoyed by barrels to benefit from the river's nutrients and currents.

Religious sites Chau Doc is home to several notable temples and pagodas, including the **Lady Xu Temple**, considered one of the holiest in southern Vietnam and named after a female statue found here in the early 1800s. Pilgrims flock to her temple in April for the **Lady Xu Festival**,

Top right Tra Su Cajuput Forest **Bottom right** Monks, Sam Mountain

JIMMY TRAN/SHUTTERSTOCK ©

Two-Million-Dollar Hill

War buffs will enjoy visiting **Tuc Dup Hill**, also known as the 'Two-Million-Dollar Hill' after the amount of money it's said the US spent on trying (and failing) to take it.

when the statue is bathed and reclothed, with bits of the discarded garments taken away as lucky charms. Head up **Sam Mountain** for more religious sites, with bonus views over the rice fields.

Cham villages On the border with Cambodia, Chau Doc is a melting pot of cultures including Chinese, Khmer and Cham. Unlike the Hindu Cham of central Vietnam, the 12,500 or so Cham people in the Mekong Delta are predominantly Sunni Muslim. Visit one of the Cham villages with their stilt homes, mosques and weaving workshops to learn more of this unique culture.

Tra Su Cajuput Forest Nature lovers will want to make a day trip to the Tra Su Cajuput Forest, 30km southwest of Chau Doc. Home to 140 types of flora and 70 species of birds, this 850-hectare ecosystem is simply magical. Cruise over a living carpet of water plants through the submerged mangrove forests, then climb the 25m-high observation tower for views over the treetops.

NGUYENQUOCTHANG/SHUTTERSTOCK ©

Listings

BEST OF THE REST

See & Do

EXO Travel

Let someone else do the planning with EXO Travel's overnight chocolate tour from Ho Chi Minh City to Can Tho, visiting cacao farms and home workshops that make all sorts of fascinating products like puffed rice and rice paper.

John's Tours

See more of Phu Quoc on land and water trips from John's Tours, covering both the north and south parts of the island, as well as on boat trips to other islands that include snorkelling and lunch.

Jerry's Jungle Tours

Led by New Zealander Jerry, these private tours get high marks for tailoring itineraries to specific requests, including birdwatching and island-hopping.

Phung Hung Fish Sauce Factory

On the way to An Thoi Port on Phu Quoc, see how fish sauce is made at the Phung Hung factory. Walk between the giant vats and breathe in the fishy goodness. There's also a shop where you can buy different grades of fish sauce to take home.

⫻ Speciality Dining

Hu Tieu Quan Ky My Tho $

An institution in My Tho, Quan Ky serves lots of variations of noodle soup, including wonton and egg noodles. But it's the My Tho–style soup for which it's famous, getting high marks for its rich broth and tangy dipping sauce.

Bun Ca Be Hai $

Plastic tables and chairs spill out onto the street at this popular local eatery specialising in Chau Doc–style fish noodle soup. The limited menu also includes fresh summer rolls, balut eggs and sweetened mung-bean milk.

Crab House $$$

Bright and modern, Crab House makes it easy for seafood lovers on Phu Quoc to feast on crab, lobster, squid and more. Simply pick your protein, sauce (including Louisiana Cajun) and spice level, and let the restaurant do the rest.

Banh Hoi Ut Dzach $$

After learning how to make delicate vermicelli rice noodles, enjoy them with grilled pork skewers in a garden setting at this Can Tho restaurant with a small noodle-making factory on site.

⫻ Markets on Land & Water

Phu Quoc Night Market

The pedestrian-only night market in Phu Quoc is a fun place to eat your way through. There

Phu Quoc Night Market

are more than 100 food stalls here, including those selling live seafood in tanks ready to be cooked to order, as well as street food and sweet treats.

Tay Do Night Market

Vendors start setting up around 4pm just across from Can Tho's Ninh Kieu Pier for the vibrant Tay Do night market, where you'll find lots of grilled food on sticks. The nearby Ninh Kieu night market sells mainly clothes and shoes.

Long Xuyen Floating Market

Off the tourist trail, this market is spread out over a 2km-long stretch of river where you'll likely be the only tourist. The boats (including anchored floating houseboats) are more spread apart, making it easier to get up close for great photos. It's on the way to Rach Gia (gateway to the island of Phu Quoc).

 Sea & Sun

Paradiso Beach Club

Paradiso is all about its location on the northern end of Sao Beach, one of Phu Quoc's prettiest. The menu is basic and not exactly cheap, but getting away from the stretch where most bus loads get dropped off is heaven.

Rory's Bar

It's worth the trip to the eastern coast of Phu Quoc to get to this Aussie-run beach bar with a mini golf course, pétanque and swimming in a natural rock pool. A DJ spins tunes on most Saturdays, and the salt-and-pepper squid is highly recommended.

 Family Fun

VinWonders Phu Quoc

Vietnam's largest theme park has more than 100 rides and games including a water park, roller-coasters, a giant aquarium and more, spread over 27 hectares.

VinWonders Phu Quoc

Khu Du Lich Lang Be

The kids will love all the folk games in this entertainment park right in between My Tho and Ben Tre – many of them involving swinging on ropes, crossing narrow bridges and balancing on beams, all above shallow ponds of water. Expect to get wet.

 On the Water

Victoria Mekong Cruises

One of the most eco-friendly ships in the delta, the luxe, all-cabin *Victoria Mekong* visits less touristed destinations on three- and four-night cruises between Can Tho in Vietnam and Phnom Penh, Cambodia. It's also one of the only cruise ships sailing out of Can Tho. The shore excursion to the Tra Su Cajuput Forest is especially delightful.

Mekong Eyes

The Mekong Eyes fleet of boats ply the waters between Ho Chi Minh City and destinations in the Mekong Delta, including Can Tho, Con Dao and Phu Quoc, or further on to Phnom Penh. There's also a completely private cruise option.

 Scan to find more things to do around the Mekong Delta online

Practicalities

ARRIVING

240

GETTING AROUND

242

SAFE TRAVEL

244

MONEY

245

RESPONSIBLE TRAVEL

246

ACCOMMODATION

248

ESSENTIALS

250

LANGUAGE

252

Right Rush hour, Ho Chi Minh City (p176)

EASY STEPS FROM THE AIRPORT TO THE CITY CENTRE

Noi Bai International Airport (Hanoi) and Tan Son Nhat International Airport (Ho Chi Minh City) are the two major gateways, though an increasing number of flights from abroad also serve Danang International Airport (Danang). All three have cafes, restaurants, shops, currency exchange, SIM card kiosks and ATMs.

AT THE AIRPORT

GRACETHANG2/SHUTTERSTOCK ©

SIM CARDS

You can buy a SIM card for an unlocked phone from one of the kiosks after baggage collection, but there are usually better deals in the city. Kiosks open sporadically; you'll usually find at least one option. Staff speak basic English; hand your phone over and ask them to register the SIM for you.

WI-FI

There is free and unlimited wi-fi in all three airports. The network usually asks for basic information like name and passport number. It disappears soon after leaving the terminal.

CURRENCY EXCHANGE

Currency exchange is usually (ie not always) available after baggage collection, but you'll find better rates in the city.

ATMs

There are always ATMs available, though not all of them always work. Visa and MasterCard are the most widely accepted.

CHARGING STATIONS

There are no charging stations, though you'll find a few wall sockets scattered around.

VISA REQUIREMENTS

Visa requirements for Vietnam are complicated, and the COVID-19 pandemic has only confused matters. Citizens of many countries can enter visa-free if they're staying for a limited number of days and they don't return to Vietnam within a set period. Otherwise, a prearranged visa or visa on arrival is necessary. Check the official tourism website (vietnam.travel) for up-to-date information. Visa-on-arrival procedures occur immediately before immigration.

GETTING TO THE CITY CENTRE

You'll need cash in Vietnamese dong for all transport options.

HOW MUCH FOR A...

bus
30,000d

motorbike taxi
100,000d

shuttle bus
80,000d

PUBLIC BUSES

Buses from the airports in Hanoi and Ho Chi Minh City are air-conditioned and comfortable. Public buses from the airport in Danang are less reliable.

GRAB

This app is Southeast Asia's Uber, and it's just as easy to use. Note that taxi drivers are given priority at airports so, while ordering a Grab is possible, you may have trouble finding the car. The price is usually a little less than a taxi.

TAXIS (Hanoi 350,000d; Ho Chi Minh City 200,000d; Danang 150,000d)
You can find taxis waiting at the ranks outside arrivals. Asking them to use the meter is usually the safest bet.

MOTORBIKE TAXIS

Motorbike taxis hang around outside the airports in Ho Chi Minh City and Danang only. You'll have to bargain hard while deploying a sense of humour.

SHUTTLE BUSES

You can take a shuttle bus operated by Vietnam Airlines or VietJet Air, Vietnam's two biggest airlines.

OTHER POINTS OF ENTRY

Land Entering overland is possible from Cambodia, Laos and China. The most popular overland journeys for travellers are by bus, and include Phnom Penh (Cambodia) to Ho Chi Minh City, Savannakhet (Laos) to Hue, and Vientiane or Luang Prabang (Laos) to Hanoi or Vinh. It's also possible to enter overland from China, usually by train or bus to Lao Cai near Sapa or bus only to Mong Cai in Quang Ninh.

Booking the entire journey is usually simpler than booking a bus to the border and trying to find onward transport. The buses will stop for a few hours while everyone gets off and moves through immigration. It's boring and inefficient, but usually not unpleasant. Make sure you have all the paperwork in order or you'll be left at the border.

Sea Arriving to Vietnam by boat is virtually unheard of, though if Phu Quoc is your first port of call, it's possible to book a bus from Sihanoukville, Kampot, Kep or even Phnom Penh to Ha Tien in southern Vietnam. From there you can catch a ferry to Phu Quoc. There are also luxury multi-day cruises from Phnom Penh to Can Tho in the Mekong Delta.

TRANSPORT TIPS TO HELP YOU GET AROUND

There are plenty of ways to travel around Vietnam. Flying is the fastest and most expensive, though it will rarely break the bank. Car hire almost always comes with a driver, which is wise considering the unfamiliar roads and way of driving. Motorbike hire is simple and affordable. Travelling by train or bus is the cheapest and slowest way to get around.

PLANES

The domestic flight network is highly developed. Most airports are served by flights from Hanoi and Ho Chi Minh City, but there are also plenty of routes between midsize cities and islands. The main airlines are Vietnam Airlines, VietJet Air and Bamboo Airways. Book tickets on airline websites.

TRAINS

Train travel is slow and the destinations limited, but it's one of the most scenic and enjoyable ways to travel. Most trains have four compartment types: hard seat, soft seat, six-berth bed and four-berth bed. The *Reunification Express* serves most coastal cities and a few inland ones. Book tickets at dsvn.vn.

HOW MUCH FOR A...

domestic flight 1,200,000d

overnight train 800,000d

overnight bus journey 300,000d

MOTORBIKING

While motorbikes are common across Southeast Asia, no other nation has embraced them quite like Vietnam. Some travellers buy them at the beginning of their trip for around 8,000,000d, take them across the country, and then sell them on before they leave. International motorbike driving licences are accepted, though you'll almost never be asked to present one. Make sure you're covered by insurance.

MOTORBIKING ESSENTIALS

Take it slow. You're on holiday; there's no need to rush.

Drive on the right but keep an eye out for one-way streets.

Indicate always, even if other people don't.

Try not to stop unless you're at traffic lights. Weave around obstacles instead.

Be mindful of all the drivers in front of you. Cutting people off is standard practice, so it's your job to predict what might happen ahead of you.

KNOW YOUR CARBON FOOTPRINT

A domestic flight from Hanoi to Ho Chi Minh City emits about 126kg of carbon dioxide per passenger. A flight from Hanoi or Ho Chi Minh City to central Vietnam would be more than half that.

PRIVATE CARS

Hiring a car is always a viable option, especially if you have fellow travellers to share the cost with. Private cars are especially suitable for half-day trips (2,000,000d), day trips (3,500,000d) and journeys of no more than a couple of hours (1,500,000d).

CYCLING

Getting around by bike is a rewarding way to see Vietnam, but be prepared for intense heat, furious rain and treacherous traffic. Unless you're an expert, consider using a company that can provide a support vehicle for your luggage.

CRUISES

Cruises that start in one destination and finish in another can sometimes be a convenient way to travel. This is only possible in Vietnam's two biggest cruise destinations: the Tonkin Gulf (which includes Halong Bay) in the north and the Mekong Delta in the south.

BUSES

Buses go everywhere and at any hour. Quality varies hugely, from air-conditioned and modern sleeper buses imported from China to ramshackle minibuses that have seen better days. You can book long-distance buses on company websites. Futa Bus and The Sinh Tourist are both reliable.

FERRIES

Ferries are useful for getting to the islands, and in some cases they're the only option. Popular journeys include Hai Phong or Halong City to Cat Ba, Cua Dai (near Hoi An) to Cu Lao Cham, and Ho Chi Minh City, Vung Tau or Soc Trang to Con Dao. Ferries to Phu Quoc run from Rach Gia and Ha Tien.

ROAD DISTANCE CHART (KM)

	Can Tho	Ho Chi Minh City	Mui Ne	Dalat	Nha Trang	Quy Nhon	Hoi An	Danang	Hue	Hanoi
Ho Chi Minh City	170									
Mui Ne	370	220								
Dalat	460	310	150							
Nha Trang	590	440	220	130						
Quy Nhon	800	620	430	340	210					
Hoi An	105	880	720	640	500	300				
Danang	1070	900	750	660	530	330	30			
Hue	1150	1000	840	750	620	420	130	100		
Hanoi	1820	1640	1500	1410	1280	1080	790	770	660	
Sapa	2140	1960	1820	1730	1590	1390	1100	1080	980	320

SAFE TRAVEL

Vietnam is a relatively safe country for travellers. There are few no-go areas, even in large cities, and violent crime against foreigners is rare. It's important to be mindful of pickpockets and bag snatchers in Ho Chi Minh City and, to a lesser extent, Hanoi.

DRIVING

The roads in Vietnam are unquestionably dangerous, but because people tend to drive slowly, accidents aren't usually fatal. Nevertheless, don't get behind the wheel (or handlebars) unless you feel confident operating the vehicle. If your driver is driving too fast, do tell them to slow down.

SWIMMING

Crowded beaches have lifeguards, but their job largely consists of sitting in chairs and using megaphones to shout at those who are swimming too far from the shore. It's better to comply, even if you feel you're being safe. As in other countries, red flags mean no swimming. On lifeguard-less beaches and in rivers, always be mindful of undercurrents.

HIKING

Climbing mountains and traversing jungles always comes with risk. There are clinics even in remote areas, but fully equipped hospitals only exist in the cities and large towns. Hospitals offering an international standard of comprehensive health care can only be found in Hanoi, Hai Phong, Danang and Ho Chi Minh City.

PICKPOCKETS & BAG SNATCHERS

These are a problem, especially in HCMC. Carry bags with straps that go over both shoulders. Drive-by phone snatching also happens; avoid pulling your phone out close to the road.

ASIA IMAGES/SHUTTERSTOCK ©

KITZCORNER/
SHUTTERSTOCK ©

INSURANCE If you go to a hospital or clinic in Vietnam, you'll have to pay upfront and claim the money back from your insurance company later. Getting a police report for theft can be a long process; be persistent.

TYPHOONS

Typhoon season is June to November. They can hit any part of the country, causing flooding in lowland areas and landslides in the mountains. There's little to no information in English, but locals know typhoons are coming days in advance. If they're advising you to leave a place, leave.

GROPING

Groping can occur in larger cities, usually at night and on quiet streets. Perpetrators typically appear on motorbikes and the crime occurs quickly and suddenly. If it happens, report it to the police.

QUICK TIPS TO HELP YOU MANAGE YOUR MONEY

CASH

Cash is king in Vietnam, so don't even think about trying to get by without it. It's always best to pay in Vietnam dong (VND). Banknotes can be confusing, so take time to familiarise yourself with them. The highest denomination is 500,000d (a little over US$20) and the lowest is 1000d (less than 5¢). There are no coins.

CURRENCY

Vietnamese dong

HOW MUCH FOR A...

Vietnamese coffee
30,000d

bowl of *pho*
45,000d

meal for two (mid-range restaurant)
300,000d

BANKS Banks exchange foreign currency at decent rates. They also offer international money transfer services like Western Union. Larger branches will usually have a member of staff who speaks English.

FOREIGN CURRENCY

Foreign money is not widely accepted, but it may be possible to use it in emergencies or for very large purchases in souvenir shops or in big hotels. USD is the easiest to use, followed by EUR. Expect an undesirable exchange rate.

BARGAINING

Possible but complicated, even for locals. Generally speaking, if the price is written down, don't haggle. If it isn't, by all means try, but check the prices in other stores or market stalls. Understandably, vendors can take offence at unreasonably low offers.

MONEY CHANGERS

These services usually offer better rates than banks and currency exchange kiosks, but you'll have to be careful not to be short-changed. There are two types: people (usually women) with wads of cash hanging around in central locations and near tourist attractions, and gold shops. Gold shops are everywhere, and how they manage to offer such competitive rates is a mystery. Some choose not to use them, believing that they are fronts for money laundering.

CREDIT CARDS

Visa and Master-Card are increasingly accepted in midrange and top-end establishments, especially in the cities. Other card types, like American Express, aren't widely accepted.

ATMS

ATMs are easy to find in cities, towns and even some villages. 2,000,000d (less than US$100) is usually the maximum you can withdraw, but you can make multiple withdrawals.

TIPPING

Tipping in Vietnam isn't expected in hotels, cafes, bars or restaurants frequented by locals. It's expected in tourist and top-end restaurants. Guides and drivers expect tips but won't be pushy about it. Massage therapists also expect tips – up to 50% of the cost is standard – and will likely be pushy. If a massage parlour doesn't allow tipping, signs will indicate this.

VIETNAM POSITIVE-IMPACT TRAVEL

TIM WEST-HEISS/SHUTTERSTOCK ©

ON THE ROAD

Calculate your carbon There are a number of online calculators. Try resurgence.org/resources/carbon-calculator.html.

Reusable bottles, cutlery and straws Make a handy eco-friendly travel kit. It's also good to get into the habit of asking for no straw when you order drinks.

Refuse plastic bags Bagging up purchased items is the norm in Vietnam. If it happens before you've had a chance to refuse a bag, simply take your items out and politely return the bag – you won't cause offence.

Wear a mask If people around you do, or if you're asked to. This simple gesture can make people feel a lot more comfortable, especially in remote areas.

Adventurous eating Eating things you wouldn't find at home is all part of the fun of travel. But think twice before eating wild animals, such as turtle.

GIVE BACK

Visit wildlife reserves and protected areas and support organisations conserving wildlife and biodiversity. Animals Asia (animalsasia. org) programmes include visiting a bear sanctuary near Hanoi. They also helped to set up an ethical elephant experience in Yok Don National Park.

Make a financial donation to children's charities that you think are doing good work. It's often more useful than donating clothes, books, food or your time. Blue Dragon (bluedragon.org), Saigon Children's Charity (saigonchildren.com) and Hue Help (huehelp.org) all have good reputations.

Be sceptical about short-term volunteering, sometimes called 'voluntourism', as it can do more harm than good. Many small charities will invite you to their office to speak about their programmes, but may be unwilling to take you on site visits, especially if children are involved.

DOS & DON'TS

Do take your shoes off before entering homes.

Do cover your shoulders when entering a temple or pagoda.

Do shake hands with one hand on your forearm to show respect.

Don't haggle unless you're confident the item is overpriced.

Do give and and receive money with two hands.

Don't sit with your back to the altar in a family home.

LEAVE A SMALL FOOTPRINT

Flights Do you really need to fly? Consider an overnight train or bus for some journeys – if you travel while asleep, you won't lose time.

Reduce your impact on nature by staying on trails in national parks and not touching trees, plants or coral.

Bring your own soap and other toiletries rather than using the little plastic bottles provided by the hotels.

Think about eating locally produced food as much as possible rather than steak from Australia or salmon from Norway.

SUPPORT LOCAL

Support social enterprises Seek out businesses giving back to their community. Koto (kotovilla. com) in Hanoi and Streets International (streets international.org) in Hoi An are good places to start.

Help small businesses Eat, stay and shop in small, family-owned establishments whenever you can. After the pandemic they'll need help more than ever.

Conserve intangible heritage Take home something meaningful by buying from artisans and artists.

CLIMATE CHANGE & TRAVEL

It's impossible to ignore the impact we have when travelling, and the importance of making changes where we can. Lonely Planet urges all travellers to engage with their travel carbon footprint. There are many carbon calculators online that allow travellers to estimate the carbon emissions generated by their journey; try resurgence.org/resources/carbon-calculator.html. Many airlines and booking sites offer travellers the option of offsetting the impact of greenhouse gas emissions by contributing to climate-friendly initiatives around the world. We continue to offset the carbon footprint of all Lonely Planet staff travel, while recognising this is a mitigation more than a solution.

RESOURCES

vietnam.travel/sustainability
env4wildlife.org
vacne.org.vn
nature.org.vn
visitquangnam.com

UNIQUE AND LOCAL WAYS TO STAY

From luxury beachside resorts to boutique city hotels, accommodation in Vietnam is good value. In most locations the range of options is similar to that of any developed tourist destination. Most hotels provide additional services, such as motorbike rental, guides and excursions. Note that category terms are used rather loosely in Vietnam: a 'boutique hotel' doesn't necessarily have only a few rooms, and an 'ecolodge' isn't always environment-friendly.

HOW MUCH FOR A...

homestay
100,000d

boutique city hotel
800,000d

five-star
beach resort
3,000,000d

CITIES

In the cities, rows of small hotels offer private rooms for all budgets, from shoestring to chic. There's also a handful of heritage hotels – historic hotels or heritage buildings repurposed as hotels – in older cities: the Sofitel Metropole in Hanoi, La Residence in Hue, Ana Mandara in Dalat and the Continental (among others) in Ho Chi Minh City.

COUNTRYSIDE

Rural lodges are rustic in appearance, consist of a set of detached bungalows and fall into midrange or top-end categories. In the north they tend to be in mountainous destinations like Sapa and Mai Chau. In the centre they might sit among rice paddies or overlook lagoons. In the south they'll be in remote corners of the Mekong Delta provinces. They're worth hunting out if your budget allows.

BEACH RESORTS

Vietnam's beaches are extraordinary; unsurprisingly, resort construction has swelled in recent years. Vietnam's most popular resort destinations are Phu Quoc and Nha Trang, but you'll find big hotels on most beaches. Quality varies wildly. You're much better off reading a few online reviews than looking at websites and photos.

and robust mosquito nets. Others leave much to be desired.

Most homestays will have some sort of social media presence, usually a Facebook page, which is a valuable place to check reviews. Rooms are shared, with compartments fashioned out of sheets and curtains. Many (but not all) homestays won't take in more than one group at a time, so you'll likely only be sharing with your fellow travellers. The price is low (usually less than 100,000d per person with breakfast), but note that the family will expect you to also pay for dinner (100,000d to 200,000d per person). For many travellers, eating with the family is one of the highlights of staying at a homestay.

HOMESTAYS

Homestays are a wonderful way to explore rural parts of Vietnam, particularly the northern mountains. They are essentially B&Bs that usually belong to members of ethnic minority groups, and you'll sleep on beds that are laid out on the floor. Homestays are always basic, though comfort can vary wildly. Some have plush mattresses, rustic bedside lighting

BOOKING

There is an overabundance of hotel rooms in Vietnam, so booking more than a few days in advance is rarely necessary. The exception is for one-of-a-kind hotels or during national holidays in popular destinations, like Hoi An. Vietnam does have high seasons – October to February for international visitors, and June to July for domestic travellers – but this shouldn't cause any issues.

Booking.com (booking.com) A good selection of places to stay, with flexible reservation options.

Agoda (agoda.com) Similar to Booking.com, and sometimes with better deals.

Airbnb (airbnb.com) An excellent selection of places to stay in Vietnam, including more unusual options. Hotels also list their rooms here.

Vietnam Coracle (vietnamcoracle.com) A superb review and booking site with honest, independent reviews.

Facebook (facebook.com) Booking over social media isn't at all unusual in Vietnam. Often all you need to do is send a message to the official hotel page, and somebody will reply in minutes. Facebook is the most common, but Instagram also works.

CBT Vietnam (cbtvietnam.com) A reliable site for booking homestays in and around Sapa.

CRUISES

Cruise destinations in Vietnam include Halong Bay and the Mekong Delta. Cruising in the south is more geared towards midrange and luxury travellers, but Halong Bay is a free-for-all. One- or two-night cruises are the most common.

ESSENTIAL NUTS-AND-BOLTS

CHEERS

If you're invited for a drink, clink glasses. But if you feel pressured to drink, you may take a small sip and politely decline more.

ADDRESSES

Though street names are generally marked, numbering can be confusing. Google pins are usually accurate.

NOISE POLLUTION

Karaoke, construction and car horns can interrupt a night's sleep, even in rural areas. Bring earplugs.

FAST FACTS

Time Zone
GMT+7

Country Code
+84

Electricity
220V 50Hz

GOOD TO KNOW

Visa regulations are in a state of constant flux. Visit vietnam.travel/plan-your-trip/visa-requirements for the most up-to-date requirements.

Local business hotels in rural areas don't have no-smoking rooms, but some rooms smell worse than others. Ask to see multiple rooms if it's a problem.

Traffic won't stop for you – even at pedestrian crossings – but they will slow down and weave around you.

Large sums of foreign currency (US$5000 and greater) must be declared at customs.

ACCESSIBLE TRAVEL

Wheelchair users will need to plan their trip carefully, as many hotels – and sometimes entire destinations – won't have considered accessibility.

Vietnamese cities are chaotic places and moving a wheelchair on sidewalks will be a challenge in most places. Some cities (Danang, Hue and Hoi An) are more wheelchair-friendly than others (Hanoi and Ho Chi Minh City).

Accessible dining outside the shopping centres is tricky, but restaurant workers will usually do what they can to help.

Vietnamese people are hospitable and not shy about offering assistance. Note that you may be on the receiving end of unsolicited help.

PAYING THE BILL

If you invite someone for a drink or meal, you should pay the bill. If someone invites you, let them pay unless they suggest splitting it.

PERSONAL QUESTIONS

Don't be offended by questions about marital status, age or weight. It's how some Vietnamese chit-chat, especially in rural areas.

MAKING FRIENDS

People may approach you wanting to practise their English. If you don't want to, simply smile and politely refuse.

FAMILY TRAVEL

Kids are adored in Vietnam, and you may find that perfect strangers often come to admire and play with your children.

If kids take a seat in a bus or train, they pay the price of a ticket; otherwise they don't.

Admission to sights is often free for kids, but the cut-off age depends on the place. If it isn't clearly signposted, ask.

SMOKING

Smoking can happen almost everywhere, including indoors, but it's polite to ask before you light up. If someone is smoking nearby and it's bothering you, it's acceptable to politely ask them to stop.

TOILETS

Most toilets are Western-style, even in rural areas. Sometimes they don't have hand soap, so it's a good idea to carry your own.

Toilet paper is not used in Vietnam. Carry your own if you're not comfortable with water.

LGBTIQ+ TRAVELLERS

Vietnamese people tend to be conservative but tolerant, though young urbanites are increasingly progressive. Same-sex couples and trans travellers are unlikely to run into problems.

Outside Hanoi and Ho Chi Minh City, Vietnamese people (regardless of sexual orientation) don't usually engage in public displays of affection.

Ho Chi Minh City has the most vibrant LGBTIQ+ scene. In Hanoi it's more understated.

The US and UK embassies host, organise and fund regular LGBTIQ+ events in Hanoi and Ho Chi Minh City.

LANGUAGE

Vietnamese pronunciation is not as hard as it may seem at first as most Vietnamese sounds also exist in English. With a bit of practice and reading our pronunciation guides as if they were English, you shouldn't have much trouble being understood.

There are six tones, indicated in the written language (and in our pronunciation guides on the right) by accent marks above or below the vowel: mid (ma), low falling (mà), low rising (mả), high broken (mã), high rising (má) and low broken (mạ). Note that the mid tone is flat. Word stress is not an issue in Vietnamese.

BASICS

Hello.	*Xin chào.*	sin jòw
Goodbye.	*Tạm biệt.*	daạm bee·ụht
Yes.	*Vâng/Dạ.* (North/South)	vuhng/yạ
No.	*Không.*	kawm
Please.	*Làm ơn.*	laàm ern
Thank you.	*Cảm ơn.*	ğaảm ern
Excuse me./ Sorry.	*Xin lỗi.*	sin lõy

What's your name?
Tên là gì?   den laà zeè

My name is ...
Tên tôi là ...   den doy laà ...

Do you speak English?
Bạn có nói được tiếng Anh không?   baạn ğó nóy đuhr·ẹrk díng aang kawm

I don't understand.
Tôi (không) hiểu.   doy (kawm) heẻ·oo

TIME & NUMBERS

What time is it? *Mấy giờ rồi?*   máy zèr zòy

It's (8) o'clock.
Bây giờ là (tám) giờ.   bay zèr laà (dúhm) zèr

morning	*buổi sáng*	boở·ee saáng
afternoon	*buổi chiều*	boở·ee jee·oò
evening	*buổi tối*	boở·ee dóy
yesterday	*hôm qua*	hawm ğwaa
today	*hôm nay*	hawm nay
tomorrow	*ngày mai*	ngày mai

1	*một*	mạwt	6	*sáu*	sóh
2	*hai*	hai	7	*bảy*	bảy
3	*ba*	baa	8	*tám*	dúhm
4	*bốn*	báwn	9	*chín*	jín
5	*năm*	nuhm	10	*mười*	muhr·eè

EMERGENCIES

Help!	*Cứu tôi!*	ğuhr·oó doy
Leave me alone!	*Thôi!*	toy

Please call a doctor.
Làm ơn gọi bác sĩ.   laàm ern gọy baák seẽ

I'm lost.
Tôi bị lạc đường.   doi beẹ laạk đuhr·èrng

Index

254

VIETNAM INDEX C-H

000 Map pages